THE LONG WALK TO CANTERBURY

The Long Walk to Canterbury

A Personal Journey

JONATHAN THORNDIKE

Edited by: Claudia Thorndike

Ingram Spark

To my mother

Contents

Author's Note

In this story about walking the Pilgrim's Way in England, I make occasional literary or historical allusions and use a few acronyms. I sometimes use "PW" (for the Pilgrim's Way), "NDW" (for the North Downs Way), "UK" (for the United Kingdom of Scotland, England, Northern Ireland, and Wales), and FEB (for the full English breakfast). Readers will find a list of books referenced at the end except for very common primary sources such as the Bible or Shakespeare's plays. I do not use footnotes or endnotes since this is not an academic book, and footnotes can interrupt the narrative. If I insert a direct quote from a published source, I include the page numbers in parentheses following the quote and give complete publication information in the list of references. If a book has entered the public domain 70 years after the author's death, I cite the original publication. *The Long Walk to Canterbury: A Personal Journey* is being sold at or below the cost to produce it. Any incidental profit will be donated to a charity: The National Trust for Places of Historic Interest or Natural Beauty with headquarters in Swindon, Wiltshire, United Kingdom.

Map of The Pilgrim's Way to Canterbury

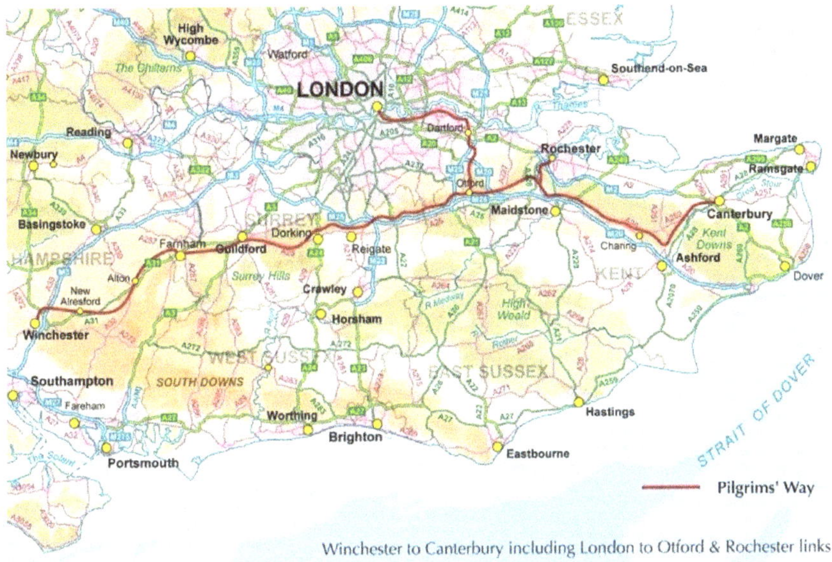

Winchester to Canterbury including London to Otford & Rochester links

The Pilgrim's Way begins in Winchester and follows a chalk ridge for 140 miles east through Hampshire, Surrey, and Kent before arriving at Canterbury Cathedral. Two alternate routes begin in Southwark, London or Rochester. The three paths meet together in Otford and end at the shrine of the Martyr St. Thomas à Becket.

Source: Leigh Hatts, *Walking The Pilgrims' Way To Canterbury from Winchester and London* (Kendal, Cumbria: Cicerone, 2017).

Chapter 1: Winchester

A Blessing and Hospital Visit

We picked up our Pilgrim's Passports in the gift shop of Winchester Cathedral before we met the Dean, Reverend Canon Dr. Roland Riem, who kindly gave us a blessing and talked with us about Canterbury before we started walking there.

We huddled inside the warm, dry, comfortable space of Winchester Cathedral in Winchester, Hampshire, United Kingdom, formally known as the Cathedral Church of the Holy Trinity, Saint Peter, Saint Paul, and Saint Swithun. Claudia and I were waiting for someone. We heard a loud voice at the south entrance asking for us. A few of the vergers or greeters (elderly parishioners who help guide worshippers and tourists) motioned over to us.

"You must be someone important to get the Dean to meet with you," a gentle gray-haired man in a red sports coat said, as we sat on simple wooden chairs.

I did not think we were important. I had contacted the church a few months ago from the States requesting a ritual send-off, and the Dean had kindly responded with an email confirmation. The Reverend Canon Dr. Roland Riem led us back to a small chapel. He leaned in close to Claudia and me. He was holding a notebook and a book of prayers for giving us a formal blessing. Before that, he chatted with us to learn why we were there. He pointed out a mosaic image of St. Ethelwold (also spelled Æthelwold) on the wall—someone I had never heard of—as apparently more important than the better-known saints, Swithun of Winchester, and Thomas à Becket of Canterbury.

The Reverend Canon Dr. Riem turned to us, saying, "If you don't mind me asking, are you walking the Pilgrim's Way to Canterbury with anyone special in mind?"

We had lost my mother a few months earlier and decided that we would dedicate this pilgrimage to her. The Reverend said a blessing to send us on our journey:

"May the grace of God and our Lord Jesus Christ be with you and keep you safe on this journey to Canterbury."

Though grateful for "Rollie" (as he was called) taking time out to visit with us and pray with us, I was not really listening to his words.

My wife and I had arrived in Winchester from Oxford and London the day before. Our first stop was at the gift shop to purchase the Pilgrim's Passport, which resembled an official US passport with quotations, shaded ink drawings, and space for stamps. The idea was to use the passport to document the journey to Canterbury. Many of the small village churches of Hampshire, Surrey, and Kent keep pilgrim tables out in the narthex, sometimes with water bottles, snacks, and greetings. The stamp is usually kept in a small box and designed with a unique image of the church or village. Sometimes it was a scavenger hunt to find the elusive stamp. The pilgrim's stamp could be kept inside a drawer, hidden in a corner of the church, or across the street in a convenience store. Maybe it was meant to take the walker's mind off the inevitable blisters, stinging nettle sores, and weary legs.

The day before, we had done a preliminary walk to the Hospital of St. Cross and Almshouse for the Noble Poor, about two miles south of Winchester along the River Itchen. Primary school kids dressed in white sweaters and pants were playing cricket alongside the path across the river. We watched them for a few minutes in what seemed like a moment of childhood fun and reverie. They were probably on a break from their school lessons.

St. Cross is called a "hospital" in the old sense of offering hospitality to deserving people. It was founded by Bishop Henry de Blois, a 12th-century monk from the Cluny Abbey in the Loire Valley, France. He was the grandson of William the Conqueror. In those days, England and France did not exist as modern nations, but the lands were closely allied through culture, religion, and various monarchs. Bishop Henry had walked the pilgrimage to Santiago after a visit to Rome; he was also a friend and supporter of Thomas à Becket. Becket became a martyr to his cause (church before state) after he defied the wishes of King Henry II, who sent knights to execute Becket on 29 December 1170 in Canterbury Cathedral.

King Henry is thought to have said, "Who shall rid me of this meddlesome priest?" Apparently, the king did not really intend his complaint as a direct execution order because in 1174, four years after the murder, he traveled to Canterbury as a barefoot pilgrim himself. The king a "humble penitent!" He was not the first but one of many walkers there drawn by Beckets' fame. King Henry felt that his words had been misinterpreted; he really did not want the charismatic Becket dead but simply resented Becket's intransigence.

Once associated with Becket's murder, Canterbury became magnetic; pilgrims walked from all over Europe to be healed, to get a drop of Becket's blood in a leaden vial, to get a blessing, to have adventure, and for a thousand other reasons. The church did not turn away from the attention because it meant tithes, increased political power, and more worshippers. Ancient Canterbury must have presented a circus-like atmosphere with all manner of hawkers, fruit and vegetable sellers, priests and monks, horse traders, relics to touch, pubs to visit, and chance encounters with the divine and miraculous.

No one can say exactly when the Pilgrim's Way originated, but historians believe that pilgrimage to Canterbury from either London or Winchester began as early as 1172. The practice grew rapidly for almost 500 years. Pilgrimage was abolished in 1534 when King Henry VIII declared himself "Supreme Head of the Church of England," severing ties with Rome and making legitimate Henry's marriage with Anne Boleyn. Before Henry VIII, such was Becket's fame that pilgrims included King Louis VII of France, Alexander II of Scotland, and King Edward I of England. Holy Roman Emperor Charles V walked to Becket's shrine in 1520, but it was soon to be destroyed by Henry during the English Reformation.

Claudia and I were not mindful of Thomas à Becket, King Henry VIII, or Bishop Henry de Blois as we walked to St. Cross. We wanted the "pilgrim's dole" given out at St. Cross to anyone who asks. Bishop Henry must have felt sympathy for anyone about to do a long walk to Canterbury as well as homeless gentlemen of the parish.

Walking to St. Cross, we saw a large rat sitting peacefully among greenery on a bridge over the river as we trundled past. The "wilderness rats" must be more civilized than their urban cousins. One of the guidebooks mentioned that people are never further than ten feet away from a rat in New York or London. Well, bless their hearts—this rat certainly looked content and non-threatening.

Upon arriving, we were met by a stately old gentleman sporting a gray beard and a blue sweater vest in the porter's lodge at St. Cross.

"Hello, we are pilgrims to Canterbury. Please give us the pilgrim's dole," I said. He quickly pulled out an unrefrigerated bottle of beer and a small container of white bread nibbles. Now, I felt like a medieval pauper who had come for "alms." The fizzy beer foamed over the edge of a rustic crockery mug with its distinctive cross. Instead of a loaf of "horse bread" and a jug of ale, we ate and drank morsels and tablespoons.

It did not matter. We were planning to stop in the William Walker pub on the way back to town, where we could get a proper pint and a good pub lunch (smoked mackerel, sardines, and potatoes with Niçoise salad). There we could celebrate the diver Walker's heroic restoration of Winchester's deteriorating foundation in the early 20th century.

Walker labored for six years to shore up the building, working six hours a day in total darkness due to the rising groundwater's murkiness. He worked underground to fortify and strengthen the Cathedral's foundations, using 25,000 bags of concrete, 115,000 concrete blocks, and thousands of bricks. Walker was presented with an award by King George V in 1912. We saw his bronze bust outside the Cathedral.

In England, they do not forget their heroes or their saints (at least the people still inclined to worship). Those remembered do not have to be religious. One night in London, we watched a bunch of young, drunken lads celebrating the woman warrior Aethelflaed (eldest child of King Alfred the Great) and her 9th century victory over the invading Danes. I cannot think of one event from history that happened in America in the 9th century.

The Hospital of St. Cross was a very strange place, as old churches go. It had the atmosphere of a nursing home mixed up with a medieval cathedral. We walked in a ghostly silence. Perhaps because of the distance from town, the place was absent of the throngs of tourists common in London, Oxford, or Winchester. There was a quiet, almost empty tearoom next to the main building, and photos of the 25 "black" and "red" brothers who lived there.

The colors reference two religious orders at St. Cross, not anything racial. The "black" brothers go back to Bishop Henry de Blois in the 12th century, wearing black robes, trencher hats, and silver Cross of Jerusalem badges. The "red" brothers, relative newcomers, were founded by Cardinal Henry Beaufort in the 15th century, and they wear claret robes, hats, and Cardinal's badges in honor of their founder. These pensioners and technically homeless people only have one requirement— to attend daily matins (morning prayer services). The brothers must be widowed or unmarried. I thought of how long the building had honored the intentions of Henry de Blois—still nominally providing support to pilgrims, vagrants, and home- less old men some 900 years later.

Now, we were pilgrims. We were not homeless, but we did not know where we were going. We would be lost many times on the way to Canterbury and Becket's shrine. We would be uttering many prayers and sometimes cursing.

We needed to visit two other important people in Winchester before we started to walk to Canterbury.

How can I write about all the saints we would encounter when I am neither Roman Catholic nor Anglican? It is probably like any imaginative journey, but one with maximum history and mysticism.

Chapter 2: Swithun and Alfred

Initial Thoughts on Pilgrimage and

Two Famous Old Men of Winchester

The simple "pilgrim's dole" offered upon request at Hospital of St. Cross, Winchester

St. Swithun's Shrine in Winchester Cathedral, the beginning of the long walk

After the visit to St. Cross Hospital, which I thought of as a kind of initiation, I pondered, what does it mean to be called a pilgrim? Nothing except a willingness to walk towards a destination. The destination was historically associated with religion but need not be exclusively so.

Can we call ourselves pilgrims? Yes, so we are, but who is going to give me the credentials, certificate, keys, or authorization to walk to Canterbury? And why walk when we could fly, drive, or take the bus or train? Is pilgrimage defined exclusively by travel or could one have an imagined or metaphorical pilgrimage? Ah, so many questions, and we would have plenty of time while walking to debate answers.

We are pilgrims. I will state the obvious: life is a journey, a path, a road. Later when we listened to a nun talking about her decision to give up secular life and join the order, she talked about "the road" to committing herself. Frequently, I am reminded of Bilbo Baggins and his simple poem in Tolkien's epic, *The Lord of the Rings*:

> The Road goes ever on and on,
> Down from the door where it began.
> Now far ahead the Road has gone,
> And I must follow, if I can,
> Pursuing it with eager feet,
> Until it joins some larger way
> Where many paths and errands meet.
> And whither then? I cannot say.

We had decided to take two weeks and walk 140 miles from Winchester to Canterbury following St. Swithun's Way, the Pilgrim's Way, and the North Downs Way. Why? I found myself wondering how we would know on which path we are walking at any one moment.

Later, I was to learn that St. Swithun's Way coincides, in places, with the Itchen Way, the Allan King Way, the Watercress Way, and other unnamed Hampshire County paths. Each "way" has its own distinctive colored plastic disc, arrow, post, or marker. Sometimes the markers are well-maintained, yet other times, they are faded, covered by greenery, or removed by farmers, requiring the walker's full attention at intersections. Deciphering and finding signage are major tasks of walking from Winchester to Canterbury as the colors and icons change frequently. Walkers might be looking for an eight-foot tall, well-positioned sturdy wooden post sign or a small sticker, plastic disc, or rock in the ground. The disc might be green, red, black, orange, or some variation of that palette, probably depending on the whims of local trail maintenance volunteers.

We decided not to download the Ordinance Survey (OS) maps on our iPhones because we had paper maps, travel books, and Google maps available on the Wi-Fi at hotels, B&Bs, and pubs. Claudia said, "I don't think we need to download the OS maps using the app," referring to a previous overseas trip that brought along an enormous cell phone bill.

We agreed that this was a good plan of action, though we questioned our reasoning many times in the coming days and weeks. The OS maps are huge, fold-out, official UK government publications with way too much information. I hoped for something like the data books available for Appalachian Trail hikers, but it turned out the large-scale OS maps were invaluable and necessary. We got lost so much despite the best efforts of two teachers who know how to read maps and calculate locations.

A typical conversation (on a rainy day) went like this as an older British couple walked past with their muddy-brown terrier:

"Hello—this was not in the forecast!"

"Yes, it's been a wet walk from Winchester."

"Welcome to Britain! This has actually been a dry month. Where are you from?"

"Nashville, Tennessee."

"Oh, I see and could tell by your twangy accent. Where are you going today?"

"We are supposed to be walking towards Alresford, but we are lost and can't find any trail markers."

One positive consequence of getting lost is constantly asking for directions from random local walkers, village residents, farmers, and other pilgrims. We found the British walkers to be universally helpful and friendly, instantly able to recognize two clueless Americans without cellular data on their phones. They would typically offer all kinds of helpful local directions and suggestions about shortcuts and recommendations for the best pub in each town.

There is a long history of walking in the United Kingdom of England, Scotland, Wales, and Northern Ireland—not surprising since people have lived in these islands since the Paleolithic or Old Stone Age. According to London's Natural History Museum, the earliest physical evidence of human settlement in Great Britain is a jaw fragment found in Kent's Cavern, Devon, estimated to be at least 40,000 years old. Industrialized transport is recent. The first steam locomotive in the UK was the Stockton and Darlington line, in County Durham in 1825 (about 200 years ago). Britons needed to walk or ride horses necessary for mobility until the invention of the railway (for at least 39,800 years!). The Ramblers and associated pedestrian or trekking groups in the UK advocating for walking paths came to life in the 19th century after villages were linked by rail.

Since walking is an accepted fact of pre-industrial life and continues to be a popular recreation, England developed a unique argot to describe pathways. A "public right of way" is a legally protected guarantee of passage to walk between map points. The Countryside and Rights of Way Act (2000) implemented the so-called "right to roam" (*jus spatiandi*) long sought by the Ramblers' Association and other non-profits. Since most people did not own land in the UK, they were forbidden from walking across open fields, fishing, or hunting on land they did not own. The long history of English absentee aristocratic land holders is the reason for the existence of the *jus spatiandi* law and the detailed walking nomenclature.

For example, sections of the Pilgrim's Way are called Footpaths, Bridleways, Byways Open to All (BOAT), or Permissive Paths. Footpaths are intended for exclusive pedestrian use and often involve stiles and wooden or metal "kissing gates" to keep out bicyclists, sheep, cows, and horses. Kissing gates are half-round hinged gates that must be swung one way to open, and the enclosure will not allow livestock through. Bridleways are for horseback riding, though walkers and cyclists may use them. A BOAT can be used by any mode of transport, even four-wheel drive cars, but often the path is too rugged for them. A Permissive Path is created when a landowner allows for public use of a pathway without formally declaring a right of way—usually through livestock pastures or fields of barley or wheat.

The British love acronyms and names, especially noticeable on any OS map with all the villages detailed. We also read about Areas of Outstanding Natural Beauty (AONBs). Much of the PW goes through AONBs, which were created by the National Parks and Access to the Countryside Act of 1949.

The point is that you have a meaning-rich destination towards which to walk, not just exercising, meandering, sauntering, or promenading. You need to get to the next village on a long walk or pilgrimage, so you have intrinsic motivation built in from the word go. No need to drive to the nearest YMCA for your daily constitutional if you are a pilgrim. To mention only a few sites of pilgrimage—Rome, Canterbury, or Santiago de Compostela for Christians, Mecca in Islam, Haridwar in

Hinduism, and the Shikoku pilgrimage in Buddhism. There are no official society entrances or credentials needed. Walking is like garlic—a naturally occurring herb or activity that is impossible to overuse. The more garlic, the better; the longer walk, the better outcome—of course in the abstract (when not soaked by torrential rains, hobbled by injury, depleted in energy, or attacked by a wild boar).

Walking is made difficult by modern transportation technology and suburban sprawl designed around the automobile (how quaint the word sounds!). In so many places in America, it's impossible to not get in a car required to drive a few blocks for a cup of joe, a dozen eggs, or a simple loaf of bread. When pedestrianism is dangerous, one must encase oneself in gas or electricity-powered metal armor to travel to the mall, the office, the school—or the grocery store. Suburban sprawl was nobody's evil intent or purposely flawed design; it just happened with rapid growth and 20th century economic boom times. Maybe the difficulty of walking today in America is partly our corporate responsibility for not giving simple human transportation enough value or forethought. No doubt, health outcomes would be improved if we regarded walking as important.

What about the good old days of riding a horse or walking to the Saturday market town? That is for historical fiction and movies.

I realize we are in a place of privilege—living in a time when it is possible to walk towards Canterbury without obligation, leaving our heavy luggage to be transported by a company towards each day's end point.

We were to begin walking the following day, but there were two important people of Winchester we needed to see first. There are luminaries aplenty with Winchester's long history, but two that stood out are St. Swithun, formerly buried outside the Cathedral, and King Alfred, whose prominent statue sits adjacent to the bridge associated with Swithun over the River Itchen. Both lived so long ago (9th century BCE) that historical documents are nonexistent, of disputed authenticity, or based on legends and folklore. However, we know that both Swithun and Alfred existed as real people and attracted followers. Folklore or not, the stories are compelling.

St. James of Camino fame is the patron of walkers and pilgrims, but many churches in Hampshire and throughout Europe are named after St. Swithun, the saint whom farmers and gardeners should petition during droughts. There are three reasons why Swithun became a person who attracted pilgrims and developed a cult following his death. Swithun was born in Winchester (capital of Alfred's ancient kingdom of Wessex) and lived from approximately 800 to 862 CE during a turbulent period of English history. Danes, Vikings, Germanic tribes, marauders, and raiders from the continent ventured back and forth, searching for land and treasure. Swithun became the seventeenth Bishop of Winchester in 852 and was an advisor to King Alfred, possibly taking him on a pilgrimage to Rome.

St. Swithun is remembered today for building his bridge, for repairing broken eggs, for being a weather prognosticator, and for a hole inside the Cathedral. Of course, weather is an eternal topic of conversation in the UK, and bridges are very important to cross rivers swollen with rain. According to legend, Swithun rebuilt Winchester's East Gate bridge. While visiting with bridge builders, Swithun noticed a poor woman who had dropped and broken her basket of eggs, and he miraculously repaired the eggs.

Another of Swithun's popular associations dates from his death in 862, when he was buried in a simple grave outside the west door of the original Saxon church (north of the present Cathedral). According to *The Catholic Encyclopedia*, on his deathbed Swithun asked that he should be buried outside the north wall of his cathedral. There, visitors could walk over his grave. Raindrops from the church roof could drop upon his bones. He would be outside, in nature, greeting people. Because more miracles were attributed to Swithun after his death, his remains were moved on 15 July 971 to a new location inside the Cathedral (away from the weather). This would enable monks and priests to monitor pilgrims and extract tributes and tithes more easily.

According to legend, a violent thunderstorm erupted to show God's dissatisfaction with moving the humble priest to a more prominent shrine inside, away from common village admirers. Swithun became the predecessor of America's Punxsutawney Phil, the large rodent in Pennsylvania that predicts the six weeks of weather following Groundhog's Day on 2 February.

15 July is known as St. Swithun's day, commemorated with a poem used to remember the weather prediction for the following weeks:

> St. Swithun's day if thou dost rain
> For forty days it will remain
> St. Swithun's day if thou be fair
> For forty days 'twill rain nae mare

A Buckinghamshire revision sounds slightly more modern, like a Limerick:

> If on St. Swithun's day it really pours
> You're better off to stay indoors

On "this scepter'd isle" of England, inundated with moisture year-round, August is the only normally dry month, so the 40 days between 15 July and 24 August are typically rain-free.

Sadly, there does not seem to be much physically left of St. Swithun in Winchester. In 1006, another bishop took Swithun's head to Canterbury, and now the head rests in

Evreux Cathedral in Normandy, France. A monk took one of Swithun's arms to the Cathedral in Stavanger, Norway. The remaining parts of him were lost when King Henry VIII destroyed the churches, martyr's shrines, repossessed land, and dissolved monasteries. Swithun is remembered inside Winchester Cathedral today with a shrine depicting sunshine and rain, and he shows up as a statue holding a bridge on the altar screen.

When monks moved Swithun's grave (against his wishes) into the Cathedral in the 11th century, it stood behind an altar screen. Pilgrims would have crawled through a "Holy Hole" (still visible today) to get closer to the saint's relics. Winchester installed the modern shrine (photo above) in 1962 to mark the 1,000-year anniversary of Swithun's death. The metallic sarcophagus features candles, raindrops, sunshine, greenery, broken eggshells, and images of St. Swithun, optimistically lifted high off the stone flooring, looking like an attempt to get the bones (if there were any) away from floods.

The other major figure of Winchester, King Alfred "the Great," is commemorated with a 17-foot-tall bronze statue near the city's medieval East Gate. Alfred rises high above the nearby river and floodplain and appears to watch out over the old city center, looking like a Victorian idealization of the mythical King Arthur, Yahweh (the Hebrew God of ancient Israel and Judah), or Thor from Norse myth with his long beard and flowing locks. British sculptor Sir William Hamo Thornycroft (1850-1925) unveiled the statue in 1899, one of his many commissioned works. The statue was installed on the 1,000-year anniversary of Alfred's death.

Today, the role of Alfred's statue seems to be to mark the center of old Winchester and to oversee tourists unloading from buses parked below.

According to *The Catholic Encyclopedia*, Alfred the Great lived from 849 to 899 CE, a bit later than St. Swithun. During King Alfred's reign, the political unit we know as England was nonexistent. West-Saxons, Mercians, and other tribes fought wars against invading Danes. Alfred ascended the throne around 878 during these invasions and tribal wars. He is known for uniting disparate tribes into the Kingdom of Wessex and ushering in a period of peace. King Alfred is also credited with military innovations, trial by jury, common laws, and the founding of Oxford University. Although these achievements are not objectively documented, they attest to Alfred's deserving the sobriquet of "Great," which was awarded to him later.

The next day, on the way out of Winchester, we would walk past Hyde Abbey Gate, thought to be King Alfred's resting place. For a great king who united the nation, the ruins of Hyde Abbey are not impressive, consisting of only a simple gateway around what appears to be a playground and disused toilets next to St. Bartholomew's church. The Abbey was destroyed in 1538 by King Henry VIII, so it is not surprising that not much remains of what might have been a lavish tomb. This reputed burial place has nothing in common with the 17-foot-tall, bronze Norse god-like Alfred looking out over shops and traffic.

What were we to make of the ancient saints and kings of England? As a walker, I am unimpressed with the legends but want to believe in something—the destination, the history, the achievements, the legacy of nation building and culture of the "mother country." The saints are generally more attractive than the kings because they seem more people-centric, but I know the church is another institution built by humans with all the corruption and flaws of the nobles and aristocrats.

The diver William Walker was known for swimming, not walking. Much closer to our time, he seems more of a true hero. Underneath Winchester Cathedral, which is still prone to flooding, there is a bronze statue of a diver, often surrounded by water. This is a fitting tribute and more poignant than anything attributed to a saint.

Chapter 3: Winchester to Alresford

The Last Person Hung for Horse Stealing in England

Claudia with multiple trail markers in a "kissing gate" on The Pilgrim's Way

Sarah Thorndike (1926-2022)

Before we started walking, we attended several churches' morning and evensong services. One was a "sung matins" service at St. Paul's Cathedral in which we sat right next to the small choir consisting of only eight men, obviously professional singers. Four countertenors surprised me with their soprano, boy choir voices that went to the rafters on John Sheppard's "Te Deum," creating tear-evoking beauty beyond description in this vast worship dome of central London. Before the service, we lit a candle for my dear departed mother, who died only three months prior. This walk would give me time to think about my mother, about growing up in a small town in Michigan, and about what she did for me, my father, my siblings, and later, my own family and children.

How long would the process of bereavement last?

In his *Analects*, ancient Chinese sage Confucius wrote that three years is the normal period of mourning following a parent's death. Some of Confucius' advice seems enigmatic while other words are directed towards our pilgrimage: "When one's parents are alive, make no distant journeys; when you travel, have a set destination. One cannot fail to know the ages of one's parents. On one hand, these are sources of happiness; on the other hand, one of fear. A child has lived for three years before he leaves his mother's arms...did you not receive three years' love from your parents? A man may have exhausted himself in nothing else, but he must do so in mourning for his parents."

I did not think exhaustion was the purpose of walking to Canterbury, but perhaps the journey would be a process of mourning my mother's death—an unavoidable truth due to the timing of this trip. We planned to do this pilgrimage for years not knowing that this month would so closely follow her passing. When walking all day, we have a lot of time to think, to process, and to pray. For what?

Earlier, at an evensong service at Brasenose College in Oxford, we listen to a woman talk about her decision to join an order of Anglican nuns. She is near 60 but looks strong, high-energy, a small, compact person, with dark hair and a faint mustache. She says it took her eight years to decide to give up "normal" life and become a nun; she had been a violin teacher before she felt a call. She visited Canterbury Cathedral and saw the empty space formerly occupied by St. Thomas's shrine (it was destroyed by Henry VIII in 1534).

"That empty space is like the hole in the world that is not occupied by God. Most people who are extremely wealthy are not happy," she says, "because they do not know God. They have an empty space at their core." She says she will spend her whole life *becoming* a nun because it is an ongoing process, never finished. Just like traveling the road—it goes on and on. You might never arrive, but perhaps that is the blessing of the road, "where many paths and errands meet/ And wither then? I cannot say."

The Pilgrim's Way has start and finish points, but one might never finish thinking about what happened during the walk.

The nun worked in Kolkata neighborhoods of extreme poverty in India, but she found many people there who were happy. She tells a story about caring for an elderly nun who had recently died; she is deeply impressed by the care given to the ailing nun by other women in her order. The attending physician said there were no bedsores or marks on the dead nun's body because of how carefully she had been tended to by her sisters. I think about my mother's final days in the nursing home and the bedsores on her legs that were an unavoidable outcome of being immobile for over a year even though she was surrounded by medical care.

Our journey begins! This is the point of departure from Winchester, having received a blessing from the Dean at the

Cathedral while ruminating on life, death, children, grand-children, and the meaning of love for one's family. I am very lucky to have Claudia on this trip, walking alongside me as she has done for 40 years. Such love and faithfulness—rare in this 21st century world of technology, turbulence, guns in so many homes, children killed while at school, road rage, need-less wars, homelessness, and poverty. Here we are in England surrounded by beauty, but it is hard to avoid thinking about the challenges facing the world today.

Leading out from Winchester, the trail is easy-peasy. No mountains, river crossings, or wild boars. Just a gentle stroll along a quiet street leading to a trail on a branch of the river. The path is overgrown in places where gaps in the tree canopy allow for abundant sunshine. Vibrant swaths of Queen Anne's lace, weeds, and nettles are obstructing the trail heading out of town.

Walking from Winchester to Alresford should have been around 10 miles, and it looked like an easy stroll on even terrain at first. We were worried that we would arrive too early! Check-in time for B&Bs is around 4:00pm (16:00 in Britain), and we could normally cover about three or four miles in one hour. We had done some serious training and long walks in the winter rains of Nashville, but we are not prepared for the variability of terrain or ease of getting lost. Often, side trips add on mileage, and we sometimes deliberately leave St. Swithun's Way to see something of interest on the horizon, such as St. Swithun's church in Martyr Worthy (with a glorious stained-glass image of Swithun) or the Shelley family chapel in Avington Park.

We had no reason to worry about early arrivals. We walk about 16 miles on the first day and we are exhausted, con-stantly losing the trail and asking for help from passers-by.

Not long after we begin our walk, we come to the first of many "pilgrim churches." Some are officially self-designated as waypoints along the Pilgrim's Way, while others just happened to be within eyesight of the trail. St. Mary's Church in Avington Park is one of several churches of stunning beauty on today's walk. After we cross through a field of barley and watch a farmer pumping 2,500 gallons of water out of the river into his water tank towed by a tractor, we see a Georgian church in the distance. The church is the only one we see in the UK that has remained unchanged since the 18th century, a time travel capsule far away from heavily traveled roads and Victorian remodeling schemes. Although the church sits on Avington Park land, it is not administered by the mansion and historically lacked the attention and funding for remodeling. The church was originally built by Margaret Brydges, Marchioness of Carnarvon (1734-1768). Outside, the building looks like a nondescript brick-walled farm building or workshop. Inside, mahogany pew boxes with tall gates hold plaques adorned with family names—the ornate pew wood supposedly came from a Spanish galleon captured in 1588 by the Duke of Effingham.

I cannot believe that church architects and builders would transport that much mahogany to a small, rural church used by one family, but no matter. I'm not a historian obsessed with factual veracity; I'm a pilgrim walking to Canterbury like one of Chaucer's characters, listening to others tell stories. This church tells a story of aristocratic families who lived in the neighborhood. Hanging in the gallery is a royal coat of arms of King George III (1771). There is a memorial to John Shelley, the brother of the poet Percy Bysshe Shelley. The Shelley family has a vault in the church graveyard.

To me, the John Shelley memorial immediately suggests Fournier's famous painting of P. B. Shelley's funeral pyre in Italy. As a boy, I saw the painting in the *World Book* encyclopedia. The image is of Shelley cremated on a pile of sticks at the beach while his friends Byron, Edward Trelawny, and Leigh Hunt watch silently. The painting portrays a gray and cloud-dense sky overhead. The watchers seem strangely detached, nonchalant in a pagan ceremony, drinking wine and glancing out over the roiling waves.

Shelley had been living in Italy for four years, exiled from his native Britain because of his controversial essays and poetry on marriage and atheism, one of which got him expelled from Oxford. He sailed to Livorno in his boat, the *Ariel*, to visit Leigh Hunt, but he drowned in a storm, never having learned to swim. Almost at once, Shelley entered the land of myth when his widow, Mary Wollstonecraft Shelley, wrote that the poet was "an angel who, imprisoned in flesh, could not adapt himself to his clay shrine and so has flown and left it." According to legend, Trelawny rescued Shelley's heart from the funeral pyre and presented it to Mary, and she kept it for the rest of her life, wrapped in the text of his poem, "Adonais," which is about the death of his poet-friend John Keats in Rome due to tuberculosis:

> The breath whose might I have invoked in song
> Descends on me; my spirit's bark is driven,
> Far from the shore, far from the trembling throng
> Whose sails were never to the Tempest given;
> The massy earth and sphered skies are riven!
> I am borne darkly, fearfully, afar;
> Whilst, burning through the inmost veil of Heaven,
> The soul of Adonais, like a star,
> Beacons from the abode where the Eternal are.

Is this the purpose of this pilgrimage—to remember those who have come before? There are three churches dedicated to St. Swithun, and others at Itchen Abbas and Itchen Stoke, before we arrive in Alresford. We stamp our passports and continue the day's journey.

The River Itchen with its many branches and wide swaths of watercress flats are everywhere to be seen. The watercress looks positively edible, salad-ready, just beneath the clear, flat streams of chalk-filtered water. Often, the path of St. Swithun's Way sits below the water line or is perched precariously between strongly flowing branches. In heavy rain, I'm sure this path goes underwater with river overflow. Beech, yew, and ash trees are everywhere, with warning signs about potentially falling, weak trees due to an insect invasion and fungus.

Looking at acres of watercress, I remember Charles Kingsley's novel *The Water-babies*, a Victorian Christian allegory about a lower-class chimney sweep named Tom who accidentally crashes from a roof into the room of a wealthy young girl. Tom is driven out of town and becomes despondent, falling into a river and drowning, whereupon fairies at St. Brendan's Island rescue him and transform Tom into a "water-baby," barely four inches tall with gills. Tom undergoes various quests and adventures in his water-baby form including rescuing his former master, the evil Mr. Grimes. When published in 1863, *The Water-babies* was extremely popular and mustered support for a British law protecting the rights of children forcibly employed as chimney sweeps.

What created this British talent for fantasy and alternate reality?

In Chaucer's *Canterbury Tales*, the pilgrims seem mostly interested in eating, drinking, laughing, sex, and satire of church powerbrokers. The abundant talent at storytelling and fantasy is already present in Chaucer's *Tales*. We do not have much time for fun and games on this walk because we are moving from 8:00am till 5:00pm or later, but we *do* have some moments of levity. Sometimes humor comes in the conversations with people we meet along the way:

"Boris, Boris, Boris, come here!" a young woman calls to a small white dog running through a barley field.

"Is your dog named after the Prime Minister?" I ask.

"No, he was a rescue and came already named, and we did not want to change his name."

"Perhaps he's more obedient than the PM."

In a village pub beer garden, we notice older men walking around what appears to be a target strung up beneath a shelter. The outdoor space is too small for archery practice and surely could not be used for firing guns. The target is large, heavily padded, with no small punctures characteristic of dart boards. In front of it, a small clay figure sits on a wooden post. Soon, patrons begin throwing heavy wooden dowels or batons. When the clay "doll" is struck and falls off the post, another man quickly returns it. This game is called "Aunt Sally," a 17th-century British pub game played only in a few rural counties near Oxford.

In 2011, an Aunt Sally World Championship took place at the Charlbury Beer Festival in Oxfordshire. I do not know why it took them almost 300 years to decide on an Aunt Sally world champion, but it has happened every year since 2011.

At the Itchen Abbas church called St. John the Baptist, we find a renovated worship space and a small table set out for pilgrims with a church pilgrim's passport stamp, bottled water, and snacks. The church has bright orange carpeting, something you might see in a home improvement store. We are greeted by a friendly staff person whose office is perched in the loft above the narthex. Perhaps the staff person is on duty and watchful because of a list of FAQs about recent renovations that we noticed in the narthex. Apparently, some parishioners complained about the modernization of an old sacred space, and the priest wrote answers explaining the necessary updates. Every church has its traditionalists or longstanding members inherently against change of any type.

"What does the town name Itchen Abbas mean?" I ask the staff person. I know the first word is the river, but what about

Abbas?" I am thinking of Mahmoud Abbas, the President of Palestine. Not a likely association here.

"Well, I do not really know, but I expect it has something to do with an abbey or an abbot who lived in the village," the woman says cheerfully.

Inside, I read a framed placard about John Hughes, the last person hung for horse stealing in England. Hughes was a vagrant, a "gypsy" who was drifting through Hampshire villages. Under an old yew tree beside the church, I read his epitaph on his tombstone: "In memory of John Hughes, who died March 19th, 1825, aged 26 years. A faithful friend, a father dear, an unfortunate husband lieth here. The Lord removed his earthly body into the realms of everlasting day." The placard states that the Rev. Robert Wright traveled to London, attempting to bail or ransom Hughes out of jail. The attempt was not successful, and the prisoner was executed, but Rev. Wright promised to bury Hughes under a yew tree at his church, where Hughes's two-year-old daughter had been buried previously. The horse thief's grave is an act of charity.

Before we get to Alresford, one last stop. St. Mary's church in Itchen Stoke, Hampshire is a creepy, dusty Victorian "jewel" built in 1866 with a tall, dark roof, stained glass, and a foot-pump organ that I play briefly. Though it wheezes like an old church lady, the organ is still in working order. Looking around, I almost expect to see the ghost of Miss Havisham from *Great Expectations* or Faulkner's Emily Grierson. Why was this church abandoned when other churches have living parishioners, staff, and services? I feel like we have stumbled into somebody's crypt. Signage states that the church is not used for worship and has been placed on an "endangered places" list vulnerable to redevelopment. The UK Churches Conservation Trust currently oversees St. Mary's church, but it looks like not much is happening except for commemorations of a Spitfire airplane that crashed nearby in the 1940s during the Battle of Britain.

We continue and sit briefly in the Cricketeers' Pub on the outskirts of town for a half-pint of energy before walking, half-dead and tired, into Alresford. It is our first day on the trail and we have two weeks of this walking ahead! Will my legs still move tomorrow?

Chapter 4: Alresford to Alton

Jane Austen and a Drop of Thomas's Blood

St. John the Baptist, Itchen Abbas, with the grave of John Hughes, the last person executed for stealing horses in England (1825)

Walking between farmer's fields towards the next clump of trees to get lost in Hampshire

I think about John Hughes's grave, under the ancient yew trees at St. John the Baptist, Itchen Abbas. I do not intend to be morbid. I do not want to focus exclusively on death. I have no personal connection with John Hughes, horse thievery, or Itchen Abbas. Yet the fact remains: we are 21st century pilgrims, walking from the purported tomb of St. Swithun, who died in the 9th century, towards the tomb of St. Thomas à Becket, who died in the 12th century. Upon arriving, medieval pilgrims might have expected miraculous cures, holy oil, a drop of Thomas's blood, a blessing, or a life-changing exchange with God. We do not expect these things.

This walk is dedicated to my mother. But with all the time spent in silence walking, I also ponder other deaths: my father, my younger brother, even our daughter, who did not die but suffered late a miscarriage this same year.

What have I to do with death and mourning? How could I possibly understand what the loss of an unborn baby feels like when I cannot even fully process the death of my mother? Confucius' three-year recommendation is starting to loom like a shelf of clouds over the mountains.

In his controversial book *Iron John*, the poet Robert Bly wrote that for a person to become fully human, he or she must, for a time, travel the road of ashes, descent, and grief. Bly used the Greek word *katabasis* to describe a symbolic, psychological descent through darkness following the death of a loved one or the experience of abandonment, abuse, or serious disappointment:

> When "katabasis" happens, a man no longer feels like a special person. He is not. One day he is in college, being fed and housed—often on someone else's money —protected by brick walls men long dead have built, and the next day he is homeless, walking the streets, looking for some way to get a meal and a bed. People

know immediately when you are falling or have fallen: doormen turn their backs, waiters sneer, no one holds the subway car door open for you (70).

I also recognize that the "wounded healer" phenomenon, as described by Carl Jung, is at work on this pilgrimage to Canterbury. Jung meant that the best insight offered by psychotherapists and counselors is due to their own experience of being wounded, betrayed, or abandoned. Recovered drug addicts and reformed alcoholics make the best counselors in those subspecialties for a reason.

Robert Bly also wrote of the "kitchen work" (a personal psychic journey) necessary to work through the grief, trauma, physical or psychic wound:

> Kitchen work means intensification...the descender makes an exit—from ordinary and respectable life—through the wound. The wound is thought of as a door. If his father abandoned him, [the person grieving] becomes abandoned; during this time, he has no house, no mother, no woman. If shame wounded him, through sexual abuse, physical beating, or by ingesting a shame-filled parent, this time, he lives the shaming out—he associates with men and women who are chronically shamed, puts himself down and out where he will be shamed fifty times a day (72).

Our pilgrimage can be seen as "kitchen work" (and we will often be thinking about food). The walk to Canterbury is the physical exponent of the internal work we are doing. I am a "person of a certain age" or as the French say, *personne d'un certain âge*. Both Claudia and I are people of a certain age. I know that the world does not need, nor will it tolerate, someone perpetually in mourning. Everyone experiences grief, death is a universal event, and grief cannot continue forever. Grief has periods, seasons, a certain expected trajectory—Ecclesiastes 3 is eloquent on this topic: "There is a time for everything, and a season for every activity under heaven:/ A time to be born and a time to die, a time to plant and a time to harvest…"

We walk towards Canterbury and St. Thomas now, in part to have a new experience and new activities, in part to travel on foot, in part to walk towards the light. There is no place else towards which to move except towards happiness by the grace of God. We have so much to be grateful for. People along the way are so kind that we feel like we have had "Guardian Angels" in Britain. We have lived wonderful lives, traveled many places, had satisfying and challenging careers, we have fully independent grown children and young grandchildren. God has blessed us in so many ways that it is unfathomable to be grumpy, depressed old people. Even so, on some days, we walk the road of ashes and descent, lost in the rain and mud while we do kitchen work. On other days, the sun shines, the chalk ridge beckons beautifully on the green horizon, and the next village appears around the bend, promising outstanding pub grub and beer.

Continuing our walk, this day has fewer stops of historical interest but beautiful rural scenery. Walking towards Bishop's Sutton, we experience landscape that would be repeated many times on the PW: gently rolling hills, a modern electric train (or the steam-powered Watercress Line heritage train) speeding past in the distance, trees marking the edges of farmer's fields, livestock, open grassland, crops of turnips, potatoes, barley, wheat, hops, and other plants unidentifiable. We walk through many kissing gates and over many stiles. One anomaly is a large solar energy "farm" with high metallic fences topped with barbed wire. Here, we must walk around the fences; security cameras are everywhere.

From Alresford, we walk through the Hampshire villages called Bishop's Sutton, Ropley, Four Marks, and Chawton (the location of Jane Austen's house) before arriving at Alton—getting lost a few times and adding miles, approximately 14 or 15 for the day. When we cross one field, we see that a farmer purposely removed signposts. Perhaps he or she needs to plow the fields or forgot about signing the agreement for a "Permissive Path."

Bishop's Sutton is scenic with its small church and cluster of brick homes. The Bishop of Winchester had once used a now demolished palace (destroyed in the English Civil War) and surrounding lands at Bishop's Sutton for hunting grounds. St. Swithun's Way is hillier and more wooded as we leave Bishop's Sutton and skirt Ropley, which has a fire-damaged church under repair. The town has just one operational business: a combination Post Office, small grocery, newsagent, tearoom, and community center. We will see this kind of creative, hybrid cooperative several times on the Pilgrim's Way. The hybrid store seems a better idea than building a new strip mall.

Leaving Bishop's Sutton, we visit Old Down Wood outside the village of Ropley. The thick forest holds many twisting paths, probably hiding robbers during the heyday of medieval pilgrimage.

We meet so many "Guardian Angels" on the Pilgrim's Way. While walking away from Ropley, we come upon several intersections with paved roads, gravel paths, two-track byways, and other bridleways and footpaths converging in a confused tangle. There are no signs or trail markers posted. Suddenly, a young man with his wife (or partner/girlfriend) came running along. We stop them and ask for directions even though they are obviously doing their exercise routine. The man knows the territory, says he used to work in London, but he now enjoys living away in the countryside. Once we explain our destination of Alton, he gives us a bunch of complicated turning instructions, which we try to follow. After another 30 minutes or so, we hear him running up behind us to correct the error of our lost sense of direction.

Bishop's Sutton and Ropley could be used as movie sets for BBC historical dramas, but what we can see of Four Marks is only a large garden center with huge greenhouses, tractors, fertilizer bags, tree and bush seedlings, and everything required by farmers or gardeners. To pilgrims, the Four Marks garden center is famous for its hamburger restaurant and huge chocolate milkshakes, which we consume to give us energy to make it to Alton. I would love for our home improvement stores at home to install ice cream shops and hamburger restaurants.

It is late in the day when we amble up through Chawton to see Jane Austen's house—she lived here for the last eight years of her life until 1817 and probably wrote novels such as *Sense and Sensibility*, *Pride and Prejudice*, and *Emma* here. Austen is thought to have read a draft of her novel *Mansfield Park* to her brother Henry Thomas Austen during a carriage journey to London. Rev. Henry Austen was a curate (a priest in his first year following ordination) in Chawton following his military career.

The sun is shining hot upon our faces, the wind is not at our backs, and the rain fails to fall soft upon our fields, so we opt for a quick visit to a 16th century pub, Greyfriars', across the street from Jane Austen's house. A little refreshment will power us forward. We have a few more miles to walk before Alton, and the last couple miles are up a High Street that does not look prosperous—lots of convenience stores, charity shops, betting outlets, cell phone repair and vaping shops. Alton does have its charming aspect—surrounding *terroir* is hop country with views of occasional "oast houses" or hop kilns. Oast houses are barns with tall, cylindrical chimneys painted white and used for drying hops with a wood fire below pushing hot air up through the conical roofing.

Alton is mentioned in the famous Domesday Book, a "great survey" of southern England completed in 1086 CE by order of King William I ("the Conqueror"). The King had sent tax collectors and surveyors to work out the location of every farm, village, town, and hamlet that might owe him dues. Given Alton's location on the Roman road from Winchester, the town was popular with pilgrims and holds on to the commercial aspect today.

At the Swan Hotel, I eat a delicious dinner of Scottish salmon, potatoes mixed with cabbage and parsnips, and spinach with Hollandaise sauce. The Swan is not the most luxurious place and not really a hotel—more of a pub with a restaurant and rooms to let. As long as we have dinner and a quiet room with a bed where we can rest our feet, we are happy!

Chapter 5: Alton to Farnham

World's Most Confusing Trail Sign

Modern Millennium Window at Church of the Assumption of the Blessed Virgin Mary, Holybourne

The Most Confusing Signpost: Four Miles or 53 Kilometers Outside of Farnham, Surrey

In the morning, we walk out of the Hampshire County town of Alton through a series of soccer (football) practice fields (pitches), where I watch children's teams practicing with parents surrounding them, yelling encouragement. One practice is at a serious stadium with artificial turf and grandstands, the first I have seen in the UK. Walking east of town is an idyllic stroll through carefully manicured green spaces, worlds away from the day's headlines about Russia's invasion of Ukraine, the rising cost of food and energy, and Boris Johnson's latest political crisis including "party-gate." Soon, we fear we have lost St. Swithun's Way again with acres of green grass fields leading up against a ridge we might have to climb. This is the last day with St. Swithun; after this, we will walk the North Downs Way National Trail (NDW) to Canterbury. The two together are known as the Pilgrim's Way, though technically we do not know the exact location of the ancient trackway, according to Derek Bright.

A few sentences about footwear—tedious I know, but such an important piece of equipment when you are walking all day, something to which Claudia would attest by the end of our hike. I am not endorsed by or receive funding from any specific footwear company. No one cares about what you wear on your feet except you, the person walking in the chosen shoes or boots, so no worries about fashion.

The revolutions in ultra-light design and running-style shoes and boots have improved quality and design by leaps and bounds. Like any fashion trend, it's a matter of experiment, trial, and blisters to discover what brand and level of lightness and support a walker needs. The weight of your pack to be carried and the kind of terrain you will walk are important factors.

I wear lightweight Keen hikers as well as Altra trail running shoes. The trail runners turn out to be too light (not enough padding) for the various size rocks we encounter, so I use the

Keen boots during the day and wear the trail runners at night. I recommend sandals or "off-duty" footwear to allow your feet to breathe and recover. You have to "love" your shoes or boots to the degree that you think they improve your strength and ability to go all day. Mind over matter, unless the shoes are impossibly heavy or ill-fitting, in which case there are plenty of outfitters and outdoor shops in larger villages along the PW that can sell you boots or shoes.

We follow the River Wey now from Hampshire into Surrey, and "waterproof" footwear is another consideration. I like to say that waterproof boots are a great idea until it rains. In a torrential, all-day rain like we would experience, the best raincoats and boots do not keep you from being soaked. Working hard, walking uphill carrying a pack, and condensation inside raingear happens regardless of the weather and rain comes in over the top of boots, so wetness is a fact of the PW lifestyle.

At Upper Froyle, four miles along the path, we come to the Holybourne Church with its Millennium Window (above) and unusual dedication to The Assumption of the Virgin Mary. Upper Froyle is another movie set village made of simple lanes, red brick walls, a village green, a church, cricket green, and pub. A church brochure notes that the building dates from the 13th century and was expanded by the Lord of the Manor, Sir Hubert Miller, a dedicated "high church" worshipper who lived in Venice, Italy for a time. When Lord Miller returned to the village, he brought back small marble religious statues (saints and biblical scenes), which are displayed under the eaves of many houses—like an outdoor, public museum of Christian icons.

There is something foreign feeling about Upper Froyle, not only due to the Italian influences imported by Hubert Miller. The brochure notes that many of the village's walls were built by French soldiers taken prisoner during the Napoleonic Wars of the early 19th century. Perhaps the captives were missing home and wanted to sneak a little *mére patrie* into England.

Inside the church, elaborate priestly vestments from Venice are displayed in a glass case. The modern stained-glass design was commissioned in the year 2000, displaying images of the Virgin Mary and Jesus, Winchester, and Canterbury—thus marking the church as a waypoint for pilgrims.

Also unavoidable outside the church is one of many war memorial crosses with soldiers' names listed, something we see at virtually every church on the PW. As an American more than 100 years later, I have a hard time appreciating the scale of loss encountered here in the world wars. The historian John Keegan puts the numerous memorials in context:

> Few French and British communities lack a memorial to the dead of the Second World War. There is one in my West Country village, a list of names carved at the foot of the funerary crucifix that stands at the cross-roads. It is, however, an addition and an afterthought. The cross itself was raised to commemorate the young men who did not return from the First World War and their number is twice that of those killed in the Second. From a population of two hundred in 1914, W. Gray, A. Lapham, W. Newton, A. Norris, C. Penn, L. Penn and W. J. White, perhaps one in four of the village's men of military age, did not come back from the front. Theirs are names found in the church registers that go back to the sixteenth century. They survive in the village today. It is not difficult to see from the evidence that the Great War brought heartbreak on a scale never known since the settlement was established by the Anglo-Saxons before the Norman Conquest and, thankfully, has not been known since. The memorial cross is, the church

apart, the only public monument the village possesses. It has its counterpart in every neighbouring village, in the county's towns, where the names multiply many times, and in the cathedral of the diocese at Salisbury. It has its counterpart, too, in every cathedral in France, in each of which will be seen a tablet bearing the inscription, "To the Glory of God and in memory of one million men of the British Empire who died in the Great War and of whom the greater number rest in France" (4).

The Great War ended a long time ago, but walkers are never finished with thinking about death on the Pilgrim's Way. Do the British or other Europeans accept death as a part of life more so than Americans, with our technology, optimism, innovations, and euphemisms? Unanswerable, I know.

Enough about death. We are tired but energized and happy as we get closer to Farnham because it marks a major waypoint in our journey, the conclusion of St. Swithun's Way.

The next village is Bentley with a Norman-tower church from the 13th century and a sunken well purported to be used by pilgrims to collect water. Jane Austen's brother Henry, mentioned earlier, was the priest in this church in 1824. The church is remarkable for the enormous yew trees with drooping branches propped up by wooden and iron staves that hide the entrance. The church brochure claims that some of these trees are 350 years old, and looking at them, I believe this to be true. The time these trees started to grow is approximately when New Amsterdam was renamed New York City by soldiers of the British Empire who captured it from the Dutch.

Getting closer to Farnham, we cross paths with a family of husband, wife, children, and grandparents—the older lady nimbly making her way on trekking poles. They all look fit and jaunty, locals familiar with the many twists and turns of St. Swithun's Way, so they help us to find Farnham and its castle.

The husband is a school administrator, and the wife works in the pharmaceutical business, sometimes traveling to North Carolina for her job. The high-school age children are very attentive to the needs of their grandmother; they look back and ask if she is okay—a sweet display of generational compassion and familial love.

The most confusing trail marker of the entire journey (photo above) shows the distance of 4 miles or 53 kilometers to Farnham. This is one of the less common eight-foot-tall signposts, unmissable, and below it is a temporary poster with the warning, "Beware Fly-tippers, We Are Watching You." I've seen this warning posted on trash bins (tips) in London but as an American, I do not have the context: fly-tipping is illegal trash disposal to avoid paying taxes or costs. "To tip" is to throw trash out the window of a moving car or leave it at a roadside.

The bigger mystery is the 53 kilometers. Did a prankster simply cover the decimal point on 5.3 kilometers? There is no obvious erasure, and 4 miles is 6.4 kilometers, so the sign maker is bad at metric conversions or else the sign shows distance from Winchester. 53 kilometers is 32 miles, and that is the approximate distance we *should* have covered since Winchester, but the city's name is not mentioned on the signpost. Mystery somewhat solved.

What matters is that we've arrived in Farnham, a much more attractive town than Alton: more prosperous, with a variety of French-influenced restaurants, pubs, and shops. The castle was built in 1138 by Bishop Henry de Blois, the same bloke who put up St. Cross Hospital, as a halfway stopping point between Winchester and London. The high street is gorgeous with its Georgian architecture and many alleyways for "mews" (stables) off the main road, a reminder of the coaching trade that flourished here in the 18th and 19th centuries. Many people stayed overnight to and from London, and all those horses and their carriages needed shelter and food, too, so the mews were built into the streetscape to give horses an alleyway to their stables. In wealthy neighborhoods of London, mews can still be found tucked away behind mansions, often along quiet cobbled lanes. They no longer keep horses in the mews, and many have been converted into flats. However, walkers in Hyde Park know that a few horses still live in London because the park includes a well-maintained sandy horse path.

We are warmly greeted at the Bush Hotel, a huge upgrade from last night's combination pub/ restaurant/ B&B in Alton. This hotel is under renovation but still features a beautiful outdoor seating patio with bar and table service. One almost feels like royalty sitting in the shade surrounded by folding striped-canvas chairs on the lawn like you see in BBC period films. Oh, to be young again, to sit under the shade tree, and to sip a gin and tonic while reading a novel! We may not be young, but we still have imagination, passion, and gratefulness for being able to stay in Farnham on the Pilgrim's Way to Canterbury.

Chapter 6: Farnham to Guildford and Chilworth

North Downs Way and Durban Bunny Chow

Paved road leading into
Guildford, Surrey

St. Martha's-On-the-Hill Church
on the Pilgrim's Way in
Guildford

It is a simple equation. Walking (or bicycling) = happiness. In Germany, for their own health, people are encouraged to get outside for 30 minutes every day despite any weather consideration. Walking is supposed to make them happy. Whenever I go for a short run, walk, or bike somewhere, I always enjoy it. In his book *Two Wheels Good*, Jody Rosen asks, "Why are bikes so much fun? Because they are not cars."

Robert McFarlane in *The Old Ways* wrote that long-distance hikers are often depressives. That is a sweeping generalization, perhaps with some degree of truth. McFarlane has written about the varied landscapes of the UK as well as explorers such as George Mallory and Ernest Shackleton. I do not know if they were depressives, and the nomenclature did not exist back then. If walking is a way to feel better, why not do it? I am prone to depressive moments but do not think of myself as clinically depressed. I enjoy sad music, books, and movies, but I can carry on with normal days' activities. I like solitude and quiet time in the woodlands. Could walking be a kind of self-care or self-medication? Walking is not a drug, but it can be a positive addiction. Programming and school curricula can be designed by public health officials and educators to encourage walking or any physical activity.

An ancient Greek philosopher famously said, "*pan metron ariston*" (all things in moderation). Do everything within the realms of normal common sense. Any idea taken to its extreme becomes insanity, even something innocuous like walking, eating garlic, or drinking water.

Quite often during our daily walks, we see groups of secondary school-aged kids with overly large backpacks. Sometimes, they sit under shade trees arguing and looking at maps, or just snacking. They look outfitted for the extremes of Polar or Himalayan exploration. We learn that they are involved in the Duke of Edinburgh Awards Program, which must be completed before the age of 25. With assistance from adults, the young people undertake community projects, work on personal development in sports, arts, interpersonal skills, live in another city, or they undertake expeditions. The DofE system bestows gold, silver, and bronze awards to those who complete projects. They must be monitored by an expert and show regular activity and commitment to the program within a timeframe of between three to eighteen months. The DofE award is considered good material for someone applying to university.

We watch a group of DofE kids getting ready to hike across a bridge out of Farnham—some of them skipping stones, eating candy, or throwing sticks into the river. Maybe not Oxford or Cambridge material but looks can deceive. Maybe one of them is the next Stephen Hawking or Rosalind Franklin.

Today is the day when we say goodbye to St. Swithun's Way and switch over to the North Downs Way (NDW). The NDW intermingles with the Pilgrim's Way for the rest of the journey to Canterbury. Because the PW is much older, it often becomes a paved roadway or gravel Jeep road between villages, so it is better to stay on the NDW, away from traffic. Common sense dictates that any ancient path between two points will follow the easiest way. Livestock and even wild animals use this same "logic" if you look at deer tracks in the forest. The deer will take the short way towards food sources or water. To conserve energy, any self-respecting wild animal will take the path of least resistance. It's easier.

The downside of the NDW versus the PW: climbing chalk ridges and hills (also called fells) away from easier paths—usually resulting in gorgeous views but more sore leg muscles! It is raining lightly as we walk out of Farnham down a paved road; cars whiz past and sometimes a driver nods his head implying, "why are these idiotic Americans walking with rucksacks on a narrow road?" We turn around, realizing that the pathway left the road some ways back.

Despite this start, the North Downs Way is much better marked than St. Swithun's Way. At least there is a large metallic sign near a roundabout marking the official NDW beginning —it runs all the way to Dover, but that is not our destination.

As the trail leads into woodland, there is a tall wooden bench carved with a giant orchid. The Countryside Agency commissioned the bench called "the North Downs Way Seat," with an inscription below: 153 miles to Dover. We are not going that far but still have about 100 miles to go (or so we hope). The mileage estimate to Dover seems off. I do not think it is that far to Dover. Farnham sign makers might paint numbers before they calibrate distances (as in the 53 km sign).

The first few miles on the NDW are comparatively easy, but we notice the Hog's Back or the true North Downs off in the distance with the A31 highway running along the top. The Hog's Back ridge reaches 500 feet above sea level at its highest point, modest by American standards but still an obstacle. Why do we use the word "downs" to describe the 100-mile-long chalk ridge from Farnham to the White Cliffs of Dover? The ridge is up-land, usually above valleys, not river bottom land. The word "downs" comes from the Anglo-Saxon word *dun,* meaning hill. Like many things in the UK, what appears to be going on is not what is really going on with that word definition.

As we walk through a nature reserve managed by the Surrey Wildlife Trust, a light rain is falling, and we put on the rain jackets obligatory to England. Puttenham is the first village about six miles away; we speed up to get somewhere dry. Puttenham has a wonderful pub, the "Good Intent" and traditional Sunday roast on offer: potatoes, parsnips, onions, carrots, garlic, and roast beef with Yorkshire pudding. The beef is very tender, reminding me of prime rib, not the rock-hard chuck roast from grandmother's kitchen. Sitting in the pub and eating a high-calorie lunch, we know we will burn it off, but still: what are we doing walking in the mud and rain? A few other hikers walk past our window because the pub is on Puttenham's high street, which doubles as the NDW.

Even in the rain, Puttenham is so picturesque that one feels transported in a time machine (no reference to H. G. Wells intended). When Aldous Huxley published the dystopian sci-fi novel *Brave New World* in 1932, he used Puttenham as a home for John "the Savage." John had read nothing but Shakespeare's plays and, disillusioned by the failures of utopian planners and his unrequited love interests, he whips himself in attempted self-purification. *Brave New World* described a future dominated by central planning and virtual reality, and the book predicted genetic engineering and test-tube babies. Families do not exist in the novel. People have sex constantly without falling in love and maintain equilibrium by taking an all-purpose drug called "soma," which keeps them satiated and happy. *Brave New World* presents a strange contrast with the romantic beauty of Puttenham in the rain.

Puttenham also has St. John the Baptist Church, which dates from around 1160 (the era of Becket's execution). Many alterations and additions have happened since then, but it thrills me to think that 12th-century pilgrims walked past this same site.

Nearing Guildford after another five miles, the rain is heavier, and we climb a steep ridge to find St. Catherine's Chapel (in ruins) and St. Martha-on-the Hill. The views from the hills above Guildford are spectacular even with thick clouds and rain. St. Catherine's Chapel is known as a "chapel of ease" because it was built in the 14th century to create a place for worship for people who did not want to walk into town. Now, it is only walls with grass and trees growing up inside. The Surrey Wildlife Trust says walkers might find an adder snake up here, though we are lucky to avoid any.

I looked forward to seeing St. Martha's again, remembering a previous day trip from London. It is one of the most stunning church locations we will see on the entire length of this walk, so dear reader, I beg your forbearance on this.

St. Martha's is fully functional and reminds me of a movie that used the church for a wedding scene: Kenneth Branagh's *In the Bleak Midwinter* (a rom-com despite its title). St. Martha's was restored in 1850 from the ruins of an earlier Saxon church. Alas, we arrive too late to get inside. Usually, rural village churches in the UK are always unlocked, but Guildford is big enough, and a commuter town for London, so it attracts some transients or potential thrill-seekers who might steal something of value.

St. Catherine's is directly on the PW and is accessed only on foot. There is an original porch that bears cross markings purportedly left by pilgrims. Had we been able to gain access, we would have seen remnants of an earlier Becket chapel and a modern stained-glass window depicting him. Legends state that on this hill high above the river, ancient pagans killed Christian martyrs, which may account for the unusual name of the church. However, the name Martha does appear in the Gospels as the sister of Lazarus, so the name might not have come from skewered early followers of Jesus.

I am not familiar with the French actress and musician Yvonne Arnaud (1890-1958), but Colin Saunders wrote that Guildford's theater is named after her. She appeared in films in the 1930s and 40s and had a long career in Britain. After she died in Guildford, Ms. Arnaud's ashes were scattered on this hill near the church, where there is a memorial tablet. I can see why she chose this as her final place of rest with this kind of scenery.

Because it is plainly visible for miles, St. Martha's was covered with large tree branches during the Second World War to remove any navigational aid to German pilots. We peer out across Tillingbourne Valley towards Blackheath (Southeast London) and the Greensand Hills as well as north towards the River Wey valley. The place reminds me of Stonehenge with its spectacular view of the Salisbury Plain in Wiltshire.

We do not go into Guildford but walk down on the other side of the hill towards Chilworth village and the Percy Arms Hotel, which reminds me of a ski lodge on the outside. Strangely, the hotel's interior decorator decided on a South African theme. The lobby displays paintings of lions and antelope, African masks, and various tartans and leather fabrics. The hotel restaurant has menu items specific to Johannesburg such as Biltong (dried meat) and Durban Bunny Chow (bread filled with curry). We both order the fish and chips. We have nothing against South Africa but want to stay English on this walk to Canterbury.

Chapter 7: Chilworth to Dorking

Charles Dickens and the Pillbox Study Group

Mr. Pickwick addresses the Club in Dickens's *The Pickwick Papers* with many scenes in Dorking; illustration by Thomas Nast (1873)

Sandwiches along the trail when no villages available for "pub grub"

You can never walk anywhere in England without literary associations. Why did this tiny island produce so many world-class writers? Maybe it's the water. Even today, British, or former Commonwealth authors demonstrate rare creative genius, intelligence, and craft in every book award category, every year. A bookseller wearing red glasses and a pink dress at Blackwell's once told me this:

"Drink a glass of water in Oxford, and you will write a book."

So it is, and here is my book. I did drink something other than beer, you see.

Today, we walk from Chilworth to Dorking, Surrey, where I look forward to the many associations with Charles Dickens, perhaps the only British author other than Shakespeare to transcend categorization. Dickens is a world unto himself. Dickens will also show up big-time when we get to Rochester. Dickens fell from favor once or twice but has now been restored, lionized, and instantly recognized by only his last name 150 years after he died. How many readers can see only one name and conjure up a universe in their minds? Dickens's characters are so deeply ingrained that they seem positively biblical: Scrooge, Bob Cratchit, Tiny Tim, Miss Havisham, Uriah Heep, Bill Sikes, Magwitch, David Copperfield, Sydney Carton, Lady Dedlock, Prince Turveydrop, Oliver Twist, the Artful Dodger, and so many more.

I owe my career in education to authors like Charles Dickens, not to mention the support of my parents, especially my mother, who was an inveterate reader and librarian. When I was in college, my favorite courses were on Beowulf, Chaucer, Shakespeare, Milton, Jane Austen, the Brontë sisters, the Romantic poets, the Victorians, Thomas Hardy, W. B. Yeats, C. S. Lewis, J. R. R. Tolkien, Virginia Woolf, and so on. I confess to writing a dissertation on the Anglo-Irish misanthrope, Jonathan Swift, and going to Ireland to dig around in the archives of Trinity College, Dublin, in the 1980s. British writers enticed me into a lifetime education career and weekend passion for bookshops, libraries, and reading.

Dickens was a frequent visitor to Dorking, and many episodes from his first novel, *The Pickwick Papers* (1836), were set in the town. Dickens based his fictional character Tony Weller, a coachman, on a prominent Dorking stable owner. In the novel, there is a Dorking pub called the Marquis of Granby (nobody knows the real identity). Tony and Sam Weller (his son) were frequent guests at the Marquis pub, where Sam makes a pilgrimage to find his mother-in-law.

Dickens always did research, absorbing names, stories, and dialects. He prowled London cemeteries and streets (sometimes at night) writing down what he heard and saw. Tony and Sam Weller in *The Pickwick Papers* speak with a pronounced Cockney dialect that Dickens picked up in London's East End —characteristically switching out the letters "w" and "v" or dropping the prefix letter "h" and the suffix "g" depending on the context.

Having trouble composing a love letter to his girlfriend in Chapter 33, Sam consults his father Tony Weller in a comedic discussion. Note the pains that Dickens takes to capture the unique qualities of the dialect:

> Sam dipped his pen into the ink to be ready for any corrections, and began with a very theatrical air—
>
> '"Lovely—"'
>
> 'Stop,' said Mr. Weller, ringing the bell. 'A double glass o' the inwariable, my dear.'
>
> 'Very well, Sir,' replied the girl; who with great quickness appeared, vanished, returned, and disappeared.
>
> 'They seem to know your ways here,' observed Sam.
>
> 'Yes,' replied his father, 'I've been here before, in my time. Go on, Sammy.'

'"Lovely creetur,"' repeated Sam.

"Tain't in poetry, is it?' interposed his father.

'No, no,' replied Sam.

'Wery glad to hear it,' said Mr. Weller. 'Poetry's un-nat'ral; no man ever talked poetry 'cept a beadle on boxin'-day, or Warren's blackin', or Rowland's oil, or some of them low fellows; never you let yourself down to talk poetry, my boy. Begin agin, Sammy.'

Mr. Weller resumed his pipe with critical solemnity, and Sam once more commenced, and read as follows:

'"Lovely creetur I feel myself a damned—"'

'That ain't proper,' said Mr. Weller, taking his pipe from his mouth.

'No; it ain't "damned,"' observed Sam, holding the letter up to the light, 'it's "shamed," there's a blot there—"I feel myself ashamed."'

'Wery good,' said Mr. Weller. 'Go on.'

'"Feel myself ashamed, and completely cir—' I forget what this here word is,' said Sam, scratching his head with the pen, in vain attempts to remember.

'Why don't you look at it, then?' inquired Mr. Weller.

'So I am a-lookin' at it,' replied Sam, 'but there's another blot. Here's a "c," and a "i," and a "d."'

'Circumwented, p'raps,' suggested Mr. Weller.

We are not reading novels today but walking (what should have been) twelve miles between Chilworth and Dorking. However, a glance at the guidebooks and maps shows a lack of villages, convenience stores like Tesco's or Sainsbury's, and pubs on today's path. A veteran walker himself of the hills of Surrey, the server at breakfast confirms a dearth of amenities on the path to Dorking. We decide on made-to-order sandwiches from the Percy Arms and hope for nothing especially South African. Is there a Pretorian chef hiding out in their kitchen?

Another deviation is our decision to walk the main road to Albury instead of ascending back up the long, steep ridge to the woods of the NDW and PW. The village of Albury is another beautifully un-modernized place (no strip malls or fast food). A strange but stately, decommissioned building awaits on the edge of town: the Catholic Apostolic Church. Although this building is no longer used, the denomination is still alive, and the building can be visited on specific days. Walking across a busy road, we ask a tradesman in his lorry (truck) about the trailhead location, and he points up the hill.

Climbing back up the ridge to the NDW, we stop for lunch, pleasantly surprised by the packed sandwiches: coronation chicken and roast beef (no Biltong). In the UK, they created special foods for the Queen's ascension to the throne in 1952, so I owe my delicious sandwich to Her Majesty Queen Elizabeth II. The hotel server and maps were correct about the lack of food stops today, though the nature reserves and abundance of trees are welcome. We see several horseback riders on the trail that seems more of a two-track gravel Jeep road, straight and flat across the spine of the ridge. Today will be less strenuous.

I still think about Charles Dickens, books, and movies as we walk. We see numerous "pillboxes," which are brick and concrete hexagon-shaped bunkhouses with panoramic views of the valleys. Small machine gun or cannon holes are the only openings allowing for light and air. The British army built many pillboxes starting in the early 1900s and added more in the 1930s and 40s. Saunders claims 28,000 were constructed all over England. But why would Germans want to invade a scenic, less populated, rural place in Surrey?

There is a "Pillbox Study Group" dedicated to the preservation of these miniature fortresses of brick that resemble the hexagonal boxes used by physicians for a patient's medicine. I wonder if they could be converted into shelters for PW walkers? In the UK, there is a club, study group, or preservation society for everything. At Bristol, the "DINOSOC" allows amateur paleontologists to continue the study of dinosaurs and fossils. Edinburgh University sponsors a chocolate society. No doubt you could be a member of both societies if you were willing to travel. In *The Road to Little Dribbling*, Bill Bryson wrote a hilarious discussion about the hundreds of heritage railway lines in the UK and their obsessive operators, who pay attention to impossibly minute details of historical accuracy.

On a related point, why are the British so good at inventing games and elaborate rules for each sport or pastime? In *Slaughterhouse Five*, Kurt Vonnegut wrote (with satiric humor) about how the British POWs were always the best at maintaining *esprit de corps* and group morale with their games and sportsmanship. So many games have British roots. In America, baseball, our national pastime, derived from cricket, football from rugby, and soccer (football here) gains in popularity every day. Watching the steeplechase event in the Olympics, one might never know its origin in the English rural landscape dotted with church steeples, fences, and puddles to jump. Living on a small, rainy island must be conducive to writing and inventing things to kick, hit, or throw to pass the time (case in point: Aunt Sally in Chapter 3). Don't get me started on the long tradition of British "athletics" (track and field) and the British mile runners like Sir Roger Bannister, Steve Ovett, Sebastian Coe, and Steve Cram.

Speaking of the modern Olympics, the official marathon distance (26 miles, 385 yards) is not actually from ancient Greece. Legends say the marathon is the route run by Pheidippides to tell the Athenians they had defeated the Persian invasion force in a fierce battle at Marathon in 490 BCE. According to the BBC, when the Olympics were held in London in 1908, there was no official length established for the marathon, which was supposed to be the distance from Marathon to Athens. The royal family requested that the marathon start at Windsor Castle and end at the royal box in the Olympic stadium so the king and his family could see it encircle Buckingham Palace.

I'm getting off the topic with all the trees and fewer villages to visit today giving me room to daydream. Pilgrimage is like life: a road to somewhere, a journey. You see something like a pillbox, and your mind makes connections you never imagined. You might or might not see others on the way. Each walker is unique. He or she might be a local with a dog running off leash, someone on horseback, an elderly couple, a serious hiker going fast, an aristocratic gent with fancy clothes and manners, or secondary school kids doing their Duke of Edinburgh programs.

We opt to bypass the village of Shere, which is supposedly very pretty but it sits a few miles away from the NDW. The guidebook author Leigh Hatts informs me that St. James's Church in Shere dates from 1190 and was used in the second Bridgett Jones movie, *The Edge of Reason* (2004). It would be the edge of unreason to add on miles to see Shere, but I would have loved to see the inside of the church and its 13th century Madonna and Child. Bridgett Jones novels and movies can be read or viewed any other time.

Descending from the ridge, we walk into Dorking on a sunny, hot afternoon and arrive at the White Horse Hotel looking like sweaty, tired horses. To my delight, the hotel has capitalized on Charles Dickens. The owner installed a hardback copy of *The Pickwick Papers* in every room instead of a Gideon's Bible. Thomas Nast illustrations hang on the walls of hallways and the dining room. I almost feel like a character in the author's imagination. Every person staying in the White Horse could be one of the thousands of characters invented by Dickens.

This has been a very long day, and we are glad to find our way into Dorking and the nice hotel. On the way, we see a statue of Ralph Vaughn Williams on the high street. He lived in Dorking from 1929 -1951 and wrote the musical setting for a church hymn, "For All the Saints," used at my mother's memorial.

Sometimes I write poems in the back of notebooks when I am trying to understand some strong emotion or memory. The Vaughn Williams statue reminds me of a poem I wrote the day after my mother passed away. I reprint it here because I like poetry, and this chapter has been so full of digressions anyway.

The Road

Life is nothing but a road—
a farmer's dirt path
through the winter wheat
where he can drive a tractor or
walk the cows towards home
and the barn's warmth or
walk to a distant church spire
piercing clouds gathered above trees.
The footpath leads down to the river
where children in summer catch frogs
and release them in the tall grass.
Bluegills in the river wait for flies
landing on water with soft ripples.
The trail, the byway open to all,
made by unknown explorers,
filled with muddy boot tracks of autumn deer hunters.
As you walk by abandoned railroad tracks,
the sun breaks through clouds
and crows call to each other in the pines,
speaking about where to find food,
their past lives, and the ghosts of friends.
You overhear two people talking,
a gentle discussion about the rain and wind.
An old wooden bridge crosses the river.

Carrying a bag of rusty gardening tools,
your hands and feet are tired at day's end.
You yearn for a pint of stout ale and
cabbage and corned beef stew.
Sitting by the fire,
you feel a hand reaching to touch your hand.
We crave knowing
who awaits in the next village,
over the next hill, who lives
in the faded white clapboard house.
What happened to old friendships
that you tasted at night like spiced wine?
The quiet of the forest,
spring snow turning into rain—
the thought of heaven.

Chapter 8: Dorking to Reigate

Sir Robert William Inglis and His Folly

Horse transport on the North Downs Way/ Pilgrim's Way in Surrey

Memorial "folly" built by Lt. Colonel Sir Robert William Inglis on Reigate Hill, a drinking fountain for horses compete with Doric columns and a star map on the ceiling for celestial navigation

I do not know what caused it—the dreaded weight gain of advancing middle age. Probably just typical for my age and sedentary profession. When I was a child, my mother said, "If you turn sideways, no one will see you. You will disappear."

I was always the tall, skinny kid in high school, over 6 feet and barely 125 pounds soaking wet. Hard to find clothes that fit my scarecrow profile. My mother was concerned about it enough to take me to a doctor in the 1960s. The doctor said I would never play football, which did not matter to me because that was something I watched on TV. He told me to eat more pancakes. I did not have any terrible disease or eating disorder. I walked, ran, and cycled everywhere in my small town and lacked patience for food preparation or eating. I did not eat much and then it was mostly grab-as-you-go, junk, and snack foods; too busy to get somewhere to wait for a proper meal of meat, potatoes, and veg. I was a good cross-country runner in high school but not a serious athlete. No matter if it+ were winter snow, spring rain, or summer heat, I was running across town to a friend's house, to the river to catch bluegills, to school, church, or to the convenience store downtown to get candy. In the deep January winter, I once ran across the frozen river carrying a single-shot Ruger .22 rifle (to the horror of my mother when she found out many years later).

Probably compounded by indolence, unacknowledged grief, and effects of the endless pandemic, I gained weight easily when my mother died. Now, I have my father's paunchy stomach and I've lost the scarecrow ability to stand in cornfields and scare birds away. I need new pants for school. Objectively, weight gain has nothing to do with my mother's death. But intuitively, I know I am no longer her tall, skinny, introverted kid who bothers his siblings and avoids responsibility. I am a person without living parents, a common fate in life as we know it.

I will not do any running on the Pilgrim's Way, but if I saw a snake, that would prompt me to hop to it. Travel books (Colin Saunders and Leigh Hatts) warn us about the UK's only poisonous snake, the adder. It is a small, stocky snake resembling a rattlesnake that lives in woodlands and moors, hunting lizards, small mammals, and ground-nesting birds such as the skylark.

Today, I see a small, dark snake slithering across the trail as we start out from Dorking. Then I recall my first year in college and another reading experience. (Is it possible that reading can be more visceral and memorable than life itself?). I took a course in Victorian literature, and we were assigned Thomas Hardy's *The Return of the Native*. In the novel, Mrs. Yeobright dies of an adder bite and is found by her son, Clym. The day before on the PW, I had stumbled through thick brambles and weeds. Suddenly, I could not see my feet but felt a heavy weight galumphing across the top of my boots. I instinctively kicked up to dislodge something, which turned out to be an old tree branch—yelp! Thank God it was no snake.

Today's walk will be shorter and easier except for a *very* steep climb up Box Hill. Before Box Hill, we walk through the Denbies Estate vineyard compound, which formerly had a 100-room mansion owned by Thomas Cubitt (1788-1855), the architect of the three Bs: Bloomsbury, Belgravia, and Buckingham Palace in London. I see no large mansion now but only miles of grape vines and men on tractors spraying them. Denbies, the largest winemaker in the UK, was fortuitously located near the site of a Roman vineyard—those ancient Romans knew how to make wine and select their *terroir* for the best results. We walk past the Bradley Farm at Denbies, which has a wine tasting center, hotel, and restaurant—but it's too early in the day for wine, and we head for the river crossing.

At dinner that evening in Reigate, we order the Denbies sparkly—not bad but not Napa Valley or French Bourgogne quality, either, in our opinion.

After walking past Denbies vineyard, we reach the ominous stepping stones, famous because they appear the only way to cross the River Mole, which leads to Box Hill. Box Hill one of the most popular family outing spots on the NDW. Box Hill is the longest and steepest ascent on the Pilgrim's Way/ NDW.

In the 2012 Summer Olympics, organizers used roads in the area for cycle road races because of the hills and curves. We can tell many people have walked around here because of the wide pathways, bridleways, and trampled dirt. The stepping stones are very tall, and the water moves past quickly, so we are glad to use trekking poles for balance. The stepping stones were removed during the Second World War (when people could not have fun) and reopened by Prime Minister Clement Atlee in 1946. The seemingly endless steps up Box Hill are under construction, but we disobey warning signs and climb anyway, zigzagging through the trees and clamoring over wooden barriers.

Luckily, there is a large visitor center at the top of the hill, and we go inside for ice cream, water, toilets, and a rest break. A young child walks through the small store, smashing bags of chips because he enjoys the noise while his mother is preoccupied with a baby in a stroller. After this entertainment, I learn from a brochure on the table that Box Hill is so named because 40% of all the box trees in Britain grow in this area.

Boxley Abbey (not here but near Maidstone, Kent, where we will be in a few days) is famous for the "Rood of Grace." The "rood" or cross was a mechanical Jesus icon with eyes and mouth that moved, manipulated by means of wires, deceiving medieval pilgrims who were stunned by the "miracle." The Boxley Abbey Jesus would roll its eyes and foam at the mouth, according to hearsay. Protestant "iconoclasts" held it up during the English Reformation as a stark example of Roman Catholics defrauding gullible peasants. The Catholic Church responded that parishioners had long seen mechanical marvels in the medieval mystery plays that toured villages.

Before we continue on our way to Reigate, I notice a "trig point" (triangulation point) near an observation platform at the visitor's center. These are lumpen concrete pillars a few feet tall. Surveyors installed 6,500 of these all over Britain to help create the OS maps, which required super-accurate measurements using sight-line mathematical calibration or triangulation. In the States, we used the same system with "benchmarks" found in wilderness areas and national parks. We have no need for trig points and benchmarks now with satellite-based GPS, but I'm sure there is a Triangulation Point Preservation Society to join if I was so moved. Serious walkers can participate in "trig bagging" or finding as many of these pillars remaining as possible.

Another common site in the area are lime kilns, tall brick chimneys used for burning limestone into "quicklime" used in farming and for making mortar for brick building projects. We see evidence of the former narrow-gauge railways used to bring chalk and limestone up to the kilns. The railways have been gone since the 1930s, so areas around Box Hill have returned to nature and the Surrey Wildlife Trust.

Our destination is Reigate and the Reigate Manor Hotel; we have the choice of climbing Colley Hill or using the road into town, which is a longer distance but flat. Claudia opts for the road, but I decide to follow a local walker who promises an outstanding view of the city (he's correct). The path is almost vertical, steps literally carved into a soft chalk hillside.

At the top, I find the Inglis Memorial (or Inglis "folly") and a memorial plaque to an American B-17 warplane that crashed and burned on return from a bombing mission to Germany. The pilot missed the tall hill, smashing his plane in a dense fog. Because of the thick woodlands and remote location, years went by before archeologists uncovered remains of the airplane and her crew. They later found living relatives of the dead airmen and brought them to England in the 1990s.

The Inglis Memorial is a strange building, a "folly" donated to the city of Reigate in 1909 by Lt. Colonel Sir Robert William Inglis. It was originally a drinking fountain for horses. Why would horses need a classical structure high above the city on a ridge that curves around a deep valley? The memorial is hexagonal, a colonnaded structure with a painted topography depicting the stars of the night sky on the ceiling. Perhaps horses need to know about celestial navigation in case they sprout wings. The surrounding land is used for grazing, so there are occasional horse and cow droppings afoot, which seems totally out of context with the Doric columns.

Perhaps this is why the Inglis Memorial is a "folly," which can mean foolishness or nonsense, as well as a Neoclassical building in a park or garden (in the archaic British sense of the word). A folly can be a small castle or temple built to satisfy the whims of an eccentric architect. Come to think of it, we still use the term in a theatrical context meaning a musical or comedy revue with elaborate costumes. All these definitions are in service to describe the Inglis Memorial, one of the most amazing sights on the 140 miles of the Pilgrim's Way.

Descending back to the road into Reigate, I realize that I have a long, hot walk to the finish line along a busy road. Claudia is nowhere to be seen, but after a few miles, a small, red car pulls up and Claudia rolls down her window, shouting "Do you want a ride?" She has found a kindly driver, another Guardian Angel, who drops both of us off at the hotel. We are both dead tired.

The Reigate Manor is a stately old place, somewhat long in the tooth, in need of redecorating, but retaining former glory with a huge, Versailles-like mirrored dining room and a pub masquerading as a book-lined study. I imagine this to be an ideal venue for wedding receptions with large-size dining rooms, dance floor, and bar. While the Denbies wine is not the best we've ever had, we do celebrate the dessert, "Eton mess," a traditional British pudding of fresh strawberries, meringue, and whipped cream layered in a tall glass. Eton mess is served at the annual cricket match between Eton and Harrow, two of England's most prestigious public (i. e. private) schools. The Duke of Wellington supposedly said, "The Battle of Waterloo was won on the fields of Eton," following his defeat of Napoleon.

As an aside, although they are known as public schools because they are open to fee-paying students regardless of place of residence, private schools in the UK are run by independent owners and are very selective and associated with the ruling classes. Government-funded schools are known as state schools in the UK.

You know, I quite like the idea of the architectural "folly." It seems so British, like something from a Monty Python sketch. Building designs are not always utilitarian—think of the Parthenon or Trafalgar Square. I have my own folly at home, a concrete bench on the side of the small garden between houses, where I sometimes sit with the Sunday newspaper. The bench serves no useful purpose and is incongruously decorated with a *fleur-de-lis*. The Inglis Memorial, with its decorations and ornaments non-useful to livestock, is the most remarkable building of the entire Pilgrim's Way. Cathedrals of course are glorious statements to the glory of God and to the history of the Church of England, but we expected those. The folly has an element of "*sprezzatura*" or "gotcha," something unexpected, whimsical, offbeat, charming, and unforgettable, like the best people we meet in England.

Chapter 9: Reigate to Tatsfield

*The Full English Breakfast, Quality Chocolates, and
The Bakery*

The full English breakfast "fry up" and a cup of coffee as we power up for walking

Gatton Park and the Millennium Stones make a halo around my head (no angel, me)

Something must be said on behalf of the "full English breakfast" or FEB, which consists of bacon, eggs, sausage, baked beans, potatoes, black pudding (blood sausage), fried mushrooms, fried tomato, and toasted bread. The traditional "fry up" gets maligned as an artificial contrivance for tourists. You see adverts for the FEB on street placards in heavily touristed areas of London.

However, according to the English Breakfast Society (yes, there is one), the FEB dates back to the 14th century, when a big breakfast feast was eaten by gentry who considered themselves guardians of traditional English agrarian customs. As recently as the 1950s, breakfast scholars estimate roughly half the population of Great Britain ate this breakfast every day! More people worked on farms in those days.

Eating this amount of food at home every morning would not help anybody maintain a healthy weight. But on the Pilgrim's Way, massive amounts of calories seem right, given the fact of walking all day long and often getting lost, not knowing when a village pub or food store will appear. How many calories are in this breakfast versus how many do we burn walking all day? Not sure. We do sometimes request substitutions in the standard FEB. I am accustomed to having oatmeal (porridge) at home mixed with fruits or other cereals, so sometimes I will request that, but just as often, I walk out in the morning having finished my "full English." I will not be hungry until mid-afternoon.

Another food-related sight in today's walk is Quality Street in Merstham village, which is a residential area of Tudor-looking homes and shops. Quality Street was a candy company originally in West Yorkshire named after J. M. Barrie's play of the same name, a Vaudeville comedy written in 1901, three years before the play that ensured Barrie's immortality, *Peter Pan* (1904). The Quality Street company sold chocolates and toffee candies well-known all over the world. Such was the play's popularity that when two London actors playing the main characters (Seymour Hicks and Ellaline Terris) moved to Merstham, the city council renamed the street after J. M. Barrie's play—not the chocolates. With an astute marketing move, the company introduced its chocolates to coincide with the release of the 1936 *Quality Street* film, which ensured wide publicity and a desire to buy sweets. PW hikers think of chocolate, not J. M. Barrie, when they see the street sign and attractive houses in Merstham.

I do like to gobble British chocolate, especially late in the day when I am getting low on energy. Cadbury's chocolates are richer and creamier than many of the kinds we can purchase at home. Along with tea, chocolate seems a necessary fact of life in England. Many stories of British explorers or soldiers mention their emergency rations with chocolate and tea included. Ah, this seems so civilized when one is in a wilderness survival mode or a battle casualty situation. Maybe I have discovered the fuel of the British Empire and its world-conquering aspirations: the full English breakfast, tea, and chocolate. Okay, and maybe British beer.

We walk through the Reigate Golf Club near Gatton Park, which makes me think of my mother again and how much she loved to play golf at the Pine River Country Club. This was her version of the British private club (in small-town Michigan) where she could play cards, join ladies' leagues, take lessons from the pro, and have meals with her friends. A great walker for all her life, she normally shunned electric golf carts and would walk for 18 holes. When she got old, she suffered from painful arthritis in her hands and legs. She had to give up golf as well as singing in the church choir because of processionals that required her to walk to the front of the church while singing. The golf club gave her an honorary life-time membership that might have meant more to her than anything the church could have done.

My mother was a 50-year church member and very active in her local church functions, but honestly, the golf club was her true spiritual home. She was not religious in a traditional sense. She looked for God in church and found Him on the golf course, you might say (pardon me for the tired cliché and well-worn male excuse).

On the trail, the area known as Gatton Park reminds us very much of a golf course with rolling hills, lakes, trees, and buildings. Gatton Park features a large "public" school, the Royal Alexandra and Albert School, many trails, lakes, and the Millennium Standing Stones. Gatton Park was the home of the Colebrooke family, who were financiers who commissioned the 18th century landscape architect Lancelot "Capability" Brown to design the place in his naturalistic style. Brown was known as "England's most famous gardener" because of his association with many country house landscape designs. In a nation obsessed with gardening, that is no mean feat.

Later, Gatton Park was purchased by Sir Jeremiah Colman, who made the famous "bull's head" spicy mustard that we love on sandwiches and bratwurst. We are lucky to have Colman's in the grocery store at home. Early in her career, Dorothy L. Sayers wrote an advert tagline for Colman's mustard: "Come on Colman's, light my fire." Sounds quite racy and ahead of Sayer's time (the 1930-40s). Sayers was a friend with and contemporary of C. S. Lewis and J. R. R. Tolkien.

The fact that I am writing mostly about food today is not lost on me—walking all day will do that. Gatton Park does have a nice kiosk where we could have bought sandwiches instead of troubling the chef at yesterday's Reigate Manor Hotel for a packed lunch—drat! The server did not know how to respond when we inquired at breakfast about buying sandwiches. A rumpled, bothered chef who looked like Gen. Bernard Law Montgomery (the irascible British General of the Second World

War) came out to interrogate us on our culinary inquiry. What unusual, never-before uttered request were we making?

The Millennium Stones (above) are worth stopping to inspect—they are permanently standing in Gatton Park now after traveling around on exhibit since their creation by the sculptor Richard Kindersley in the late 1990s. Kindersley was inspired to replicate Stonehenge but in modern terms to celebrate the double millennium of the year 2,000 AD (or CE). Each of the ten stones represents 200-year increments since the birth of Christ. They are inscribed with artful quotations from St. John's Gospel, St. Augustine, Boethius, John Scotus Erigena, St. Anselm, Shakespeare, St. Thomas Aquinas, St. Francis of Sales, Goethe, and T. S. Eliot. The first inscription reads, "In the beginning was the Word, and the Word was God."

The UK does have a thing for stone circles with Stonehenge, Avebury, and Brodgar in Orkney, Scotland, to name a few. Will Stonehenge or the Millennium Standing Stones be around a thousand years hence? Will human civilization still be around to celebrate the third or fourth millennia in the year 3,000 or 4,000 CE?

The walk to Tatsfield is very long, around 16 miles, and the travel books mention this is the highest elevation we will achieve on either the Pilgrim's Way or North Downs Way. Though we lack rest breaks in famous churches on today's walk, we do have chocolate and a fateful association with Tatsfield: Donald Maclean and Guy Burgess, two of the "Cambridge Five" British spies for Russia, stayed in Tatsfield before defecting to the Soviet Union in 1951. Maclean and Burgess passed military and government secrets to Moscow and would have faced charges of treason and execution as traitors had they remained in the UK. Why would I know about them? Ben McIntyre and his excellent research into Second World War-era espionage. I assigned McIntyre's book, *A Spy Among Friends,* about the ultimate traitor, Kim Philby, in a college writing course.

We keep a lookout in case we meet any Russian spies on the trail today. We do come upon another "folly," this time a tall, crumbling brick tower that resembles a Norman church structure called "Whitehill Tower." When I first see the tower with one side open and bricks tumbled down, I wonder, why would anyone build a church away from the village on the edge of a farmer's field? Whereas most Norman churches are from the 14th century, this tower was built in recent times (1862) by a local farmer as a memorial to his son, who was lost at sea. Like a true British architectural folly, Whitehill Tower has no useful purpose except perhaps as a statement of love.

Just before Tatsfield, we stop at a parking lot where an old man sits in his little white car with a dog, a gray-haired miniature Schnauzer. He has lost most of his teeth, has awfully long fingernails, long greasy hair, and is difficult to understand, but he does point out antique airplanes flying overhead—probably Hawker Hurricanes or Spitfires taking people for a joyride. We ask him about the availability of water, and he offers some out of his car trunk (boot). This guy looks like he lives in his car. We thank him for the offer but set off again after a short rest break.

The Bakery (our B&B) in Tatsfield is one of the few buildings around the village square, and it was literally a bakery before renovations converted it. I wonder about the wisdom of not changing the name of the B&B, if they are trying to attract customers from London who need an overnight stay (excluding Russian spies). A large, framed photo in the entryway shows when the previous owner tried to burn the building down to claim insurance money. The Bakery is a two-story, white painted and half-timbered structure that resembles a ship with a tall wheelhouse jutting into the high street. To add to confusion, the pub across the street is named "Ye Olde Ship," but it looks more like a hardware store filled with locals who call out to each other as a new person enters: "Oi, you finally got off your bum to come in for a pint?"

Perhaps Maclean and Burgess selected Tatsfield for their getaway rendezvous with their handler to escape to Russia because of these identity confusions. Is this building a ship or a bakery or a hotel? Despite its attractiveness, Tatsfield is rather generic, unremarkable, and easy to confuse with a million similar places. At dinner, a silent wine steward comes around to take our drinks order, and we notice he looks like the man in a nearby painting with two small boys.

At breakfast the following day, we learn he is the owner of the Bakery, and he traded his office job in London for a chance to run a country B&B. In fact, we could see the London skyline far across a field, twenty miles distant, when we began the approach towards Tatsfield. The Bakery owner is divorced, which we infer from the lack of a spouse in the painting. Not being an expert in interior design, I still notice a decidedly "manly" style to the paintings and framed posters inside the dining room. The breakfast food is very filling, the usual FEB, so we are ready to take on the English weather and terrain.

Chapter 10: Tatsfield to Wrotham

Duck Pond Roundabout

St. Bartholomew's, Otford with its car roundabout, duckpond, and duck house in the village center

Wrotham Village sign with images of rural English life

Today's destination is Wrotham in Kent. We learn it is pronounced "Root-um," but no one can explain why. If you tell people you are walking to Wrotham ("Roth-um"), they will say, "Where is that? Oh, it's Root-um." This was also the case a few years ago when we visited the windswept moorlands of West Yorkshire to see the village home of the Brontë sisters Charlotte, Emily, and Anne. Like the Inglis' Folly in Reigate, the Brontë sisters' home has much to do with the setting. The Brontë family made their home at Haworth, but the name is pronounced "Hooth." It is a lonely village high on a steep hill. On the way there, train travelers must pass through Keighley, pronounced "Keeth-lee." Of course, we think of Bicester in Oxfordshire ("Bister"), Magdalen College ("Maudlin"), and Gloucester ("Gloster").

You need the correct pronunciation of Gloucester for the Mother Goose rhyme:

> Doctor Foster went to Gloucester
> In a shower of rain;
> He stepped in a puddle,
> Right up to his middle,
> And never went there again.

At breakfast, we notice a light rain falling, and the maps tell us we have another sixteen-mile day ahead, so we decide to take a taxi ride and start walking a few miles east in Knockholt village to knock off a few miles. The village name sounds Germanic to me. Starting in Knockholt will allow us to avoid walking along a busy stretch of the M-25 motorway. At least this is one village with no mysterious pronunciation.

The driver of the taxi, a blue Peugeot wagon, zips quickly along curvy and narrow country lanes, crashing through wayside tree branches and sloshing through puddles at 50 mph. I am afraid a horse or tractor will come into view around a bend.

"This is a slow and lonely road," he says, but the drive seems busy and fast to walkers used to a maximum 2 mph pace. Walking on such roads is one of the dangers of the North Downs Way or Pilgrim's Way when it diverts around a large estate.

I am dizzy after the car ride. This reminds me of how lucky we are to be able to walk like medieval pilgrims and take our time over the 140 miles. Okay, medieval peasants did not have the creature comforts we enjoy, but we are still literally, in some places, walking on the same path used by people who wanted to walk to St. Thomas à Becket in the 13th century.

Today, we move from Surrey into Kent County, so you might say we have entered the final trimester of the walk. Kent is the "garden" of England because of its varieties of apples, pears, plums, cherries, vineyards, and 42 different kinds of nuts grown here. During earlier summer trips to London, we always enjoyed a side trip to see the Kent countryside and to buy fresh cherries and raspberries.

We still have many miles to walk to Canterbury, but more references to St. Thomas à Becket have started to appear in village churches. We are getting closer to the end point of our long walk. Then again, maybe it is more accurate (and obvious) to say the physical destination is not the same thing as the non-tangible benefits of this long journey. We have been given space and time to think without the normal chatter and noise of TV, mobile phones, computer screens, and road traffic.

We see the first NDW milestone, which looks like a tombstone (with an acorn carving) telling us that we are 60 miles from Farnham with 54 miles to Canterbury or 65 miles to Dover. These numbers are not correct according to the guidebooks, but no matter.

I sometimes try to imagine what medieval people thought about while walking to Canterbury. The previous day in the church of St. Peter and Paul in Chaldon, we saw a famous 12th-century mural on the west wall is known as a "Doom," a genre of Last Judgment-style paintings. This "Doom" was hidden for centuries, only uncovered in 1870 during church restorations. Perhaps later church leaders were embarrassed or afraid of the painting's message. Theologically, the Victorians were light-years removed from the pre-Reformation pilgrims of Chaucer's time. In the painting, torments of hell are shown with demons boiling sinners in a cauldron or sawing them in half. One drunken pilgrim is depicted holding an empty bottle. That would be the typical pilgrim today. The archangel Michael weighs souls while Christ waits at the top of a ladder. After the murder of Becket, pilgrims carved a letter "T" for Thomas on a pillar in this church, so we know the church was on the ancient route.

What were medieval pilgrims thinking when they saw this red and white painting of demons, damnation, and the "ladder of salvation?" Did they assume they would be "saved" if they made it to Thomas's tomb in Canterbury and received a drop of his blood or a blessing? Chaucer would have commented here on clerics like the Pardoner, who sells indulgences or forgiveness of sins, for a price. In Philippians 2: 12, the Apostle Paul instructed people to "continue to work out your salvation with fear and trembling." This painting perhaps instilled some fear in those ancient pilgrims.

After passing the two estate mansions of Titsey and Chevening, we keep walking to Otford and St. Bartholomew's Church. Otford is famous for its duck roundabout in the village center complete with duck house. We can see the mansions far across the way, but we do not want to take the time to go off the trail to visit them. The families that built the mansions are long gone, and Titsey and Chevening are owned by public trusts that allow visitors on specified days, but we are not here for Downton Abbey-like experiences. Claudia is having blister problems, so she waits on a bench by St. Bart's while I go to chat with a local chemist (pharmacist).

St. Thomas à Becket is associated with Otford because before being appointed archbishop, he served as a deacon at St. Bartholomew's. The travel books do not say whether Becket brought the ducks or not, but he did stay in the attached manor house in 1162 before moving to Canterbury. Legends claim that Becket struck the ground with his crosier to produce water at Becket's Well, so perhaps the ducks followed the flowing water, which wound up in the roundabout.

We do not take the side trip to Kemsing village, but Leigh Hatts notes ominously that the four knights who murdered Becket rode through there on the way to Canterbury. The Church of St. Mary the Virgin in Kemsing is said to be haunted by the ghost of one of the murderers. The ghost is a knight in full armor who clanks into the church, kneels, and prays at the altar every year on 29 December. That sounds like something right out of Charles Dickens's imagination -- a predecessor to Jacob Marley.

Otford is where the Pilgrim's Way route from London joins the Winchester route, and we do see a few more walkers. Chaucer's pilgrims leaving from the Tabard Inn in Southwark would have traveled the old Roman road (Watling Street). The two routes converge at Otford and south of Rochester across the Medway River.

Before we reach Wrotham, we ascend to a high ridge where I meet a group of six men wearing backpacks who are pilgrims to Canterbury. This all seems very serious and pious. Claudia waits on a bench while I join the men walking towards a viewpoint with a large cross on a brick pedestal. The cross looks as though it has been there since the First World War, one of the numerous reminders of that catastrophe that killed a generation of Europe's young men.

At first, I wonder if these six men are going to get on bended knees to pray like pious monks, but it is soon obvious they are jokesters and constantly laughing and good-naturedly harassing each other. One of them is Scottish, and when I talk about a trip to Edinburgh, they say, "Why would anyone go there? There's nothing to see in such a dismal, depressing armpit," instantly welcoming me in their merriment. They are all mid-career gents with children in the same primary school, a fun and enjoyable bunch that we will see again still laughing it up in the pub of our B&B in Wrotham. C. S. Lewis in *The Four Loves* explains this kind of camaraderie very well in his chapter on friendship.

The village of Wrotham dates to the 8th century and was a market town, but since the construction of the M-20 and M-26 motorways, the population has declined. People are more willing to drive a distance to get to bigger shops and malls rather than the quaint local stores. Wrotham's St. George's church is large and impressive, a testament to the former importance of the town. The Wrotham church is believed to be the first in England named after the country's patron saint who slew the dragon demanding human sacrifices each year. We do not see any sign of human sacrifice inside the church, but we do get our pilgrim's passports stamped.

Our B&B is called the Bull, and the pamphlet says there has been a pub and inn here since 1280 when Wrotham's Old Palace was used by archbishops going to and from Canterbury. Historians believe Becket stayed for a night in Wrotham on his final trip from London less than two weeks before his murder. I feel confident that we will not be murdered here, and tomorrow we will walk to Rochester, which should be about thirteen miles.

Chapter 11: Wrotham to Rochester

The Cuxton Angel and Don Vincenzo

Scallop shell associated with St. William of Perth and the Camino de Santiago

Rochester Cathedral was founded by St. Augustine in 604 CE and the present building dates from 1080

Today's destination is Rochester, the only city-sized place we encounter outside of our starting and ending points, Winchester, and Canterbury. Rochester is a major city and county seat, but in England, city status is rarely granted by the government and usually connected with a special anniversary. King Henry III wrote the first Royal Charter authorizing Rochester's status in 1227, but the city lost population and its city status since. Now, Rochester is merely a large town. As a part of the Queen's Diamond Jubilee in 2012, Chelmsford, St. Asaph, and Perth were awarded the city designation, which was stripped away from poor, old Rochester.

Rochester is famous because of its cathedral, which was a site of pilgrimage (apart from Canterbury). Rochester Cathedral is glorious, and another place from which people could start walking to Canterbury instead of from London. Like all European cathedrals, photographers cannot capture the building in a way to convey its majesty and grandeur. (Dear reader, to get an appreciation in place of seeing Rochester Cathedral in person, please borrow and read Ken Follett's nearly 1,000-page novel *The Pillars of the Earth*).

As always, there are literary connections with the city. In Charlotte Brontë's *Jane Eyre*, Rochester (first name Edward) is the classic "Byronic hero:" dark, brooding, romantic, mysterious, and nursing some hidden psychological wound from deep in his past. The character Rochester is an object of fascination, disgust, and desire. This seems a fitting description of the city. The city seems to be suffering from the burden of history.

At breakfast in the Bull B&B before we leave Wrotham, I notice large black and white photos framed and hung around the walls. Some photos show various types of British fighter and bomber aircraft of the 1930s and 40s. Other photos are of Royal Air Force (RAF) cadets training during the Second World War. I have read many history books about Prime Minister

Winston Churchill and the Blitz, but I have never seen anything like one unusual photo: RAF cadets riding bicycles. The cadets are riding in a line that snakes behind the leader; all the bicycles have miniature wings affixed atop the handlebars to approximate a small airplane. It looks like a children's game. The leader of the line of cycles has a smoke-making machine attached to his bike. It looks as though the cadets are playing at a dogfight or squadron maneuver behind a wounded, burning bicycle. A far cry from the computerized flight simulators available today.

As a cyclist myself, I understand the feeling of flying that riding a bike can simulate. Going fast downhill, cyclists can feel airborne. But there is something pathetic about the old photo as I contemplate it while eating my eggs, bacon, and toast.

The RAF cadets in this photo will not be ready to fight or fly Spitfires against the German Stuka dive-bombers. Maybe nothing could really prepare the young Brits for the "fog" of war, though the smoke machine tries. It seems Britain will never forget the time of its "finest hour" and defense of the homeland against a planned Nazi invasion. The British have every reason to honor their history, which is long and glorious.

In 1940 during a crisis with government ministers, some of whom were asking for peace negotiations with Hitler, Churchill famously said, "If this long island story of ours is to end at last, let it end only when each one of us lies choking in his own blood upon the ground." The Prime Minister inspired a nation with his vivid, defiant words of resistance. The victory over tyranny cannot be forgotten, a lesson so appropriate to Eastern Europe today with the Russian invasion of Ukraine. Churchill won the war in part through his soaring oratory, according to Erik Larsen in *The Splendid and the Vile*. England and the Allies also won the war because of American military prowess (with hard lessons learned in battle) and our massive industrial output. In my home state of Michigan, engineers transformed car factories overnight into producing killing machines on an unimaginable scale.

However, I also feel that England is sometimes neurotic, obsessed with the past to an unhealthy degree. There is so much history to know in Britain, and everyone should study the past, but history can become a burden or produce what Harold Bloom called "the anxiety of influence." Bloom wrote not on war but about the psychological burden new poets feel overcoming anxiety posed by the magnificent achievements of past authors. How do you write anything in the shadows of Shakespeare, Milton, Dickens, the Brontës, or Jane Austen?

As Americans, we have the blessing (or curse) of living in a "new" country, at least from the perspective of modern, industrial society. Walking through the many beautiful, virtually unchanged villages of Southeast England on the way to Canterbury, I wonder about the lives of young people. Do they feel burdened by the history of the United Kingdom, which is itself a political fiction? Would a teenager in Wrotham or Tatsfield feel there were new opportunities or potential for growth and change? First-hand impressions tell me young people would have to leave their villages and move to London, Birmingham, or Manchester for jobs or education—unless they want to become farmers, shopkeepers, or lorry drivers.

Charles Dickens spent his childhood in Rochester and nearby Chatham. He moved there as a boy when his father, a clerk in the Royal Navy office, was transferred to Chatham Dockyards. Dickens's father pointed towards an elegant house in Chatham, (Gad's Hill Place) and told his son, "If you were to be very preserving and were to work hard, you might someday come to live in it." The old "pull yourself up by your own bootstraps" school of parenting. (Note that the British like to name their houses).

As a child, Dickens was sent to a boot blacking factory when his father went to debtor's prison, the ultimate moral disgrace for Victorians, but he did eventually achieve the fame and fortune that allowed him to go back and purchase Gad's Hill Place in 1856. Ah, psychological or karmic revenge! Some scholars feel that Dickens never completely overcame the humiliation of the Victorian workhouse; it is the wellspring of his indelible characters like Oliver Twist and David Copperfield. Many Rochester buildings carry historical markers detailing their appearance in Dickens's novels; local graveyards have tombstones with some of Dickens's chosen character names. Rochester's Bull Inn shows up in *Great Expectations*, and the Eastgate House can be found in *The Mystery of Edwin Drood.*

Heading out the door of the Bull B&B in Wrotham, rain starts falling mid-morning, and it picks up intensity to give us a full-on soaking by lunch. The best rain gear and "waterproof" footwear do not keep us dry in an all-day walk through the North Downs of Kent. Soon we are chilled to the bone, possibly warding off hypothermia, teeth chattering and fingers turning blue. We must keep walking to stay warm and make progress towards Rochester. Walking through the massive Ranscombe Farm Reserve, we see a fiery, pointy-tailed orange fox sprinting for cover across a field; soon near the trail we find the half-eaten skeletal carcass of a baby lamb, head intact and still attached to its backbone. The rain is a source of life especially on a farm, and you are never far from life or death on a farm.

Slogging through an enormous vineyard, we search for the village of Cuxton and a dry place for lunch. The village is a ways down a busy lane, but luckily, we see a man clearing debris from his drains in his front garden.

"Hello, can you tell us if there is a pub in Cuxton?" I shout.

"Yes, it's about a mile down the road. You are obviously pilgrims. Why don't I give you a ride?"

"That is so kind of you, but we are muddy and wet and don't want to mess up your interior."

"No worries," he says. "I've a farm vehicle used for just such purposes."

The man is another shining example of generosity and kindness shown to strangers, the golden rule of all religions. Or else we look like pathetic American tourists in the rain. Pilgrims do tend to bring out the best in other people. We should all be pilgrims at some point in our lives. But pilgrims are sometimes viewed with derision as parasites or religious fanatics.

Some cultures honor pilgrims. In the four stages of life of Hinduism, the last stage is *sannyasa,* the process of renouncing worldly possessions and wandering from place to place, begging for food. I do not want to beg, and I have money for food, but I am cold. The Cuxton man tells us he runs a small B&B and hosts walkers on the Pilgrim's Way, so he knows our situation. Before long, he pulls up in the car park of the White Hart pub and points out the local rail terminal. Another Guardian Angel has granted us mercy.

"I tell you what—go and have a nice lunch, and then you have the option of walking down the hill and taking the local train one stop into Rochester or else walking across the Medway bridge."

We did not realize how close we were to the city.

I feel self-conscious in my fully soaked hiking clothes as I sit on a leather bench in the pub and peruse the menu—I order the special savory pie with lamb, peas, potatoes, and carrots, please, and a big pot of tea. This is an agricultural town, so no doubt that muddy farmers have been here, but I still cringe at leaving a dark water stain on the leather.

The local train quickly gets us across the River Medway and into downtown. I am glad we decided to take the train the last two miles because the bridge is traffic-heavy, a four-lane carriageway with a footpath hundreds of feet above the roiling waters. Linguists believe the river name was first recorded as *Meduwain* in 764 CE, a corruption of ancient Celtic words meaning "golden river." The Medway is broad and deep enough for large ships.

Until 1946, the Rochester riverfront was used for "flying boat" take-offs and landings. Huge airplanes with boat-like hulls and pontoons were built before the construction of jumbo jets and large international airports. Airplane engineers of the 1930s thought the future of long-haul travel involved flying boats that could go anywhere in the world where there was water. That would be two-thirds of the planet.

Unfortunately, the local train station is still a couple miles walk from our Rochester B&B called the Botleigh Villa, a poetic name. We ask for a taxi but are told they only arrive by local phone inquiry. We do not have cell phone service, and the ticket counter lady says it is an hour-long wait, so we decide to keep walking through the town. At least the rain has stopped. We are dead tired, again.

That night, we attempt a physical self-revival and attend an evensong service in Rochester Cathedral. The church altar is covered with 5,000 metal leaves as part of an art installation, a reflective memorial to lives lost during the pandemic. Each leaf is engraved with the word "hope," but they are gradually turning brown with oxidation (like real maple leaves fallen from trees). Perhaps the artist is trying to remind us that suffering, sickness, and death happen despite the hope that faith in God can bring – or conversely, that hope is always there, despite suffering, sickness, and death. We get our Pilgrim's Passports signed at the gift shop. Pilgrims from London were regular visitors here beginning in the 12th century, and the stone steps of one staircase show the deep indentation from wear and tear of hundreds of years of walkers.

Rochester Cathedral has its own local saint like St. Swithun of Winchester: William of Perth. Not originally from Rochester,

St. William was a pilgrim from Scotland who was horribly murdered just outside the city in 1201. A pious churchgoer, he was on his way to Canterbury to the new Becket shrine. He might have wanted to continue to Jerusalem. Legends say St. Will had been a baker (or perhaps a fisherman) who set aside loaves for the poor, and he decided to visit sacred sites on pilgrimage with his adopted son David, who shockingly betrayed William and murdered him. His corpse was discovered by a psychotic woman who was miraculously cured when she touched the body. The monks brought the body to Rochester Cathedral, where St. William was honored as a martyr because he had been killed while on pilgrimage and was known for his generosity to the poor.

Another famous cleric associated with Rochester Cathedral is St. John Fisher, a bishop and cardinal whose support for Catherine of Aragon caused him to quarrel with King Henry VIII. When the king learned that the church had awarded Fisher a red *galero* and named him a cardinal, the king said Fisher would never keep his head long enough to wear his red hat. The king executed Fisher on 22 June 1535, the year after he declared himself Supreme Head of the Church of England and broke with Rome. Fisher's head was stuck on a pike on London Bridge as a warning—lesson learned! Do not cross the king, especially on matters of sex, love, and marriage.

After the service, we stumble in exhaustion down Rochester's main restaurant avenue, looking for pizza. Instead, with luck we find Don Vincenzo's restaurant, which seems imported directly from the streets of Rome, Venice, or Naples. All the staff are very Mediterranean in appearance and speak with a charming Italian accent. The owner himself, a gregarious and happy person, makes his way around the sparkling-clean restaurant, checking on customers who delight in fresh rigatoni, unique homemade ravioli, and hearty red wines. The Cuxton Guardian Angel with the car, the Rochester Cathedral evensong with beautiful music and liturgy, and Don Vincenzo's restaurant gave us the perfect ending to a difficult day of rain-soaked misery.

Chapter 12: Rochester to Thurnham

Kit's Coty and the Bridal Suite

Kit's Coty House is not a house but an entryway to a Neolithic burial chamber

Even with our trusty OS maps and the road signs, we still managed to get lost on the Pilgrim's Way or the North Downs Way frequently

Our overnight accommodation in Rochester, an attractive two-story Georgian brick townhouse called Botleigh Villa, is very close in style to staying in someone's home. Botleigh Villa is a B&B but very much a personal space more than a hotel. I was afraid of opening the door to someone's private toilet or picking up the wrong socks or underwear by mistake. David and Noreen are excellent hosts and great cooks, but they seem to live in separate parts of the house. Perhaps they are amicably separated and only collaborate on a retirement business. We breakfast with another American couple who are hikers from Oregon, and it is nice to share stories of the trail.

When we describe the Pilgrim's Way and our experiences in Church of England services and struggles to follow the liturgy, the Oregonians want to change the subject, perhaps afraid we were about to evangelize. They need not have worried on that account. The word "pilgrimage" probably has different connotations to different people, and religion and politics are two topics in which it is prudent to tread lightly in today's world.

Noreen learned of Claudia's ongoing blister problems and kindly takes her to a nearby chemist (pharmacist), who gives her the same antiseptic ointment I had purchased in Otford near the duck pond roundabout. In England, the chemist can dispense medicines and give general medical advice without involving a visit to the National Health Service hospital. Maybe Claudia would be healed if we make it to Canterbury and she petitions St. Thomas for a miracle.

After my mother died, I needed to visit doctors and dentists for my own physical infirmities—root canal pain, squamous cell carcinoma removal, varicose vein treatment, and a colonoscopy. I received weekly reminders in the mail or emails about medical expenses, co-pays not covered by insurance needing payment. During the previous two years, I spent a regular amount of time each week on my mother's medical billing when she lived in a nursing home.

Now it was my turn to decipher all the different insurance and medical systems. The Roman goddess *Fortuna* had swung her debits around to my side of the table, and now I would be the recipient of medical attention. The medieval wheel of fortune had spun around to remind me of mortality and health challenges faced by any person of a certain age.

In *The Canterbury Tales*, Chaucer's monk tells the story about how great heroes such as Samson, Hercules, or Julius Caesar were brought to their knees through their inevitable decline and through *Fortuna's* fickle mood swings. In Percy Bysshe Shelley's sonnet "Ozymandias," the narrator describes the rubble of a formerly enormous statue of a fallen king who thought he was invincible. The pedestal is carved with an un-intentionally ironic inscription: "Look on my works, ye Mighty, and despair." Ha, ha king, there are no "works." King Ozymandias was probably not the laughing type, especially with his own crumbled empire on display.

What would King Henry VIII think of his works in England today?

Another one of those universals—birth, babyhood, youth, adulthood, career, marriage, parenthood, grandparenthood, decline, death. Life is a road, a journey, a pilgrimage to somewhere. Let the strong person have confidence in the ultimate destination. Let each of us in our own good time be with his or her God, god, goddess, or creative spirit. We took a small amount of my mother's cremated remains to the beach in South Carolina when we traveled there for a family vacation. Along with the columbarium at church, this was her destination, her physical pilgrimage end. She loved beach vacations with far-flung family who reunited only at such times. At our own little beach memorial service, I took the jar of ashes and flung them across sand at low tide, remembering the poet Shelley's cremation in Italy. Without success in withholding emotion, I recited in halting fashion the words of Ecclesiastes 3, 1-8:

There is a time for everything, and a season for every activity under heaven:
a time to be born and a time to die, a time to plant and a time to harvest,
a time to kill and a time to heal, a time to tear down and a time to build,
a time to weep and a time to laugh, a time to mourn and a time to dance,
a time to scatter stones and a time to gather them,
a time to embrace and a time to refrain,
a time to search and a time to give up, a time to keep and a time to throw away,
a time to tear and a time to mend, a time to be silent and a time to speak,
a time to love and a time to hate, a time for war and a time for peace.

The writer of Ecclesiastes could have been a priest or prophet for the fickle Roman goddess, *Fortuna.*

Claudia decides to take the day off from walking to allow her wounded foot time to recover, so I will be solo hiking today. I ask the driver to drop me off at Nashenden Farm outside of Rochester, so I do not have to hump my way back through the sizable city. Nashenden is not an operating commercial farm, but a nature reserve purchased ten years ago by Kent County with the aim of restoring the land to nurture habitats for native birds, animals, and plants. The land still looks farm-like, but I can see woodlands and grasslands starting to become more robust and healthier near the borders. Saunders writes that the chalk-soil is perfect for wild Kent plants: salad burnet, bird's foot trefoil, horseshoe vetch, fairy flax, pyramidal orchid, bee orchid, false brome grass, hairy violet, and bulbous buttercup. Even the botanicals in England have literary-quality names.

Looking at the map, I find an alternate trail that runs parallel to the Eurostar rail track for a mile or two before veering off up a hill towards Burham Common and the Robin Hood pub. High-speed trains whiz past me like a nuclear hurricane three times per hour. I am not very close but can still feel how trains create an air vacuum as they pass. The trains are so fast that it is impossible to read any signage or numbers on the carriages. This is the ultimate juxtaposition: me in medieval-style pedestrian pilgrimage mode paired with the hypersonic Eurostar bullet-train. What are the passengers thinking about while they whip from London St. Pancras station through the Chunnel to Paris or Brussels? I doubt that anyone on the fast train is worried about having two liters of water for a hot uphill hike. But some of them probably lost a family member in recent weeks or months.

Still worried about my choice of the alternate trail away from the NDW or PW, I ask a friendly passing cyclist about the location of the Robin Hood. It is too early in the day for lunch or a pint of ale, but the pub still serves as a well-known "trig-point" for navigation. He is riding a mountain bike and after giving directions, he says he must get back to take his children to school. Thank God for children who need to go to school!

There are many remarkable viewpoints and diversions on today's walk such as Kit's Coty House, a neolithic burial site near Aylesford. Not much remains of Kit's Coty House, which was probably once an entrance to a vast burial vault. It is not really a house but more of a huge stone post and lintel shelter looking like it was built by the Cyclopes from Homer's *Odyssey*. Archeologists say a long, chambered barrow (burial mound) here goes back to 4,000 BCE.

In Tolkien's *The Lord of the Rings*, the barrow-wights are creepy, cold spiritual beings that capture four Hobbits and try to take them into their tunnels. Kit's Coty is also the name of a nearby village thought to reference the Celtic chieftain Catigern (Kit), son of Vortigern, who died in a battle with the Saxons in 455 CE. The "coty" part of the name derives from slang for cottage. Whatever it is called, Kit's Coty is strangely serene on the top of a broad grassland overlooking a broad, scenic valley.

In a small country with a long history, walkers find memorials everywhere, whether they be graves, Neolithic burial mounds, churches, shrines, stone circles like Stonehenge, or roadside memorial crosses. The death memorials are possibly just as numerous as literary references in England. Just before Detling, I cross a busy highway at "Jade's Crossing," a special elevated walkway with elaborate ramps and stairs that looks out of place amidst the Victorian cottages. Jade's Crossing reminds me of a pedestrian crossing in Nashville high above busy Hillsboro Road on Vanderbilt's campus. Jade's Crossing is another memorial, named after a young girl called Jade Hobbs who was killed walking over the street with her grandmother. Two other people had been killed here by fast-moving traffic at the same crossing. Four pedestrian fatalities motivated locals to raise funds for the enclosed, bomb-proof steel walkway.

Another remarkable memorial not mentioned in any guidebook is the E. F. Schumacher and William Blake resting place on the trail, complete with pilgrim bench, placards, water bottles, books, and notices of meetings. Schumacher was an economist of human-scale development best known for his people-centered book, *Small is Beautiful: Economics as if People Mattered*. William Blake was an 18th century Romantic poet and printmaker who wrote stunning, prophetic epics and lyrical poems and crafted iconic engravings for many books. Both Schumacher and Blake were revolutionaries.

What good or bad is fomented by the prophets? I ask myself. Both Blake and Schumacher railed against the exploitive damages of industry and capitalism. The memorial was built by someone in Schumacher's family who wanted his words remembered. I sit on the stone bench inscribed with a slogan: "Know that your god is within, express true gratitude for what you have, and your prayers will be answered."

A little bit off, not as good as the golden rule, but still some wisdom evident. One hundred years hence, will anyone remember Schumacher or Blake? The person who constructed this shaded, peaceful rest spot wanted that to be so. I think that because there are too many, the hand-printed placards will repel the walker's curiosity. Still, I am amazed that someone went to this length to preserve, protect, and propagate the legacy of two influential British people.

People will remember Blake's poem "Jerusalem" because when it was set to music by Sir Hubert Perry, it became the unofficial national anthem of England—even including the lines, "And was Jerusalem builded here/ Among these dark Satanic Mills?" Blake was not a fan of the industrial revolution. "Jerusalem" along with "God Save the Queen" are traditionally sung at the last Proms concert every summer in London at the Royal Albert Hall. Blake's poem was only a preface to his 4,500-line epic *Milton: A Poem in Two Books.* William Blake's poem asks a question without answering: did a youthful Jesus, accompanied by Joseph of Arimathea, ever visit "this green and pleasant land?" Sir Edward Elgar composed the soaring orchestration of this hymn tune so loved even today.

Because Claudia gets to Thurnham early in the day because of taking the taxi ride, the Black Horse Inn upgrades our room to the "bridal suite!" Claudia has a nice bottle of local merlot in a decanter waiting when I arrive. The room is a lucky turn of fortune—appropriate because today is our anniversary day! Claudia decided to marry me 39 years ago, and we are still in love. We listen to people congregated in a noisy wedding reception right outside our windows while we talk dinner plans. The newlyweds sit in the center of a group of others who shout encouragement, list glasses in toasts, sing songs, and laugh. Will they leave us in peace before it is time for dinner or sleep? Will the couple outside recently united in holy matrimony still be together in 40 years?

The restaurant/pub at the Black Horse Inn is festooned with dried hops hanging from the ceiling, tipping its hat to the local farmer's product. I worry about the fire hazard. The Black Horse is too remote and inconsequential to have any regular fire inspector visits. Ironically, a sign on the wall reads, "In case of fire, please pay promptly." Even more strange are the guests in the pub who seem to have walked off a movie set —pirates, motorcycle gang members, prostitutes, Rolls Royce society aristocrats, clowns, cowboys—I do not know what else. Many people seem to be in costume and character, so perhaps there is a local film, amateur drama, or motorcycle rally. Walking down the road on the last stretch into Thurnham earlier, I watched someone in a paramotor contraption (flying lawn chair) buzzing along, high above fields of hops and barley. The flying chair has a colorful parachute or wing keeping it aloft; the pilot probably thinks lofty, ethereal ideas with his panoramic view.

What a day this has been. How could anyone be so happy and blessed as I am, walking into a scenic rural village on pilgrimage in Britain? I know who waits: a beautiful wife who loves me and still finds me attractive in my advancing years. I love her, both of us still faithful and content after so many years. Who could have deserved such a blessing? The day's conclusion reminds me of a passage from *The Four Loves* by C. S. Lewis. Lewis writes of male camaraderie here, but it still captures the mood:

Those are the golden sessions; when four or five of us after a hard day's walk have come to our inn; when our slippers are on, our feet spread out toward the blaze and our drinks are at our elbows; when the whole world, and something beyond the world, opens itself to our minds as we talk; and no one has any claim on or any responsibility for another, but all are freemen and equals as if we had first met an hour ago, while at the same time an Affection mellowed by the years enfolds us. Life—natural life—has no better gift to give. Who could have deserved it? (105).

Chapter 13: Thurnham to Lenham

Brother Percival and the Lenham Cross

The Lenham hotel references a blood sport favored by King Henry VIII; bears were chained and attacked by dogs for entertainment

Brother Percival near Harrietsham, a wooden sculpture of an exhausted monk on pilgrimage who sleeps on a bench. I gave him my hat to wear

Thurnham has a beautiful old Norman church that we wanted to visit called St. Mary the Virgin, but the obvious direction is blocked by a barrier because it passes by a luxury hotel or estate. We could walk around the long way to the other side of town, but we want to get going to Leeds Castle. Our destination is the village of Lenham, but we decide to taxi to Leeds Castle first and walk from there instead of from Thurnham. Deprived of a castle or church visit in Thurnham, we would be "castled" to the max at Leeds.

We are so close to Canterbury that we can taste it. A 30-minute taxi or train ride would whisk us there, but speed is not our purpose. I need patience, my least favorite virtue, and one most lacking in my character. I am always early to everything and impatient with anyone who is not. I lose my temper sometimes with people who have not planned or pre-pared way in advance, or who do not complete things early. It is not good to be too early or obsessed with over-preparation. There is even a word for this: "pre-crastination," coined by David Rosenbaum, a professor of psychology at the University of California, Riverside. Rosenbaum defined pre-crastination as the obsession with completing goals at the earliest oppor-tunity, even when waiting for the right moment would be more effective or achieve the best desired outcome.

Alas, Leeds would be the only strategic disappointment of the long walk to Canterbury. The day's walking distance is reduced by a small amount, which is good, and we do not get lost on the trail, but we are lost in a swarm of people at Leeds. After many days of very rural scenery and sparsely populated villages and farms, we are thrown in with a cloud of baby strollers, families with young children, tourists, and all manner of bus-trip visitors from London out for a day of scenery.

I do not mean to complain. We are on holiday to "this green and pleasant land," and the best part of the day is yet to come.

Leeds Castle's architectural beauty and landscape design is first-rate, but castles do not fit into our walk "theme." Medieval pilgrims to Canterbury would never have been here to visit with royals. Leeds was the private property of six English queens including the wife of King Edward I, Eleanor of Castile, Spain, whose name is probably the inspiration for the London Tube station with the strange name, "Elephant and Castle." King Henry VIII used Leeds as a place to keep his first wife, Catherine of Aragon, so he could get it on with Anne Boleyn, thus instigating the split with Rome and the creation of the Church of England and British Reformation. Becket, where were you when England needed a voice of reform?

There must be a reason why Leeds Castle is confusingly not located in Leeds, West Yorkshire, but in Maidstone, Kent. This geography nomenclature reminds me of the old pre-TSA joke when the foreign visitor goes to an American airport, asks for a ticket to Dulles, and is sent to Dallas-Fort Worth International.

Leeds Castle's final private owner before it became property of the National Trust (thus a tourist magnet) was Lady Baille, an American heiress. In the 1930s, Lady Baille spent a large part of her fortune restoring the castle, which had fallen into disrepair because it had not been lived in for years.

Leeds has been described as "the loveliest castle in the world" with its photogenic location surrounded by water, park-like golf course lawns, and woods. It certainly is lovely. Many films and TV shows have been shot here. The castle looks as though it comes from a writer's dream, straight from the pages of a medieval romance, surrounded by shimmering water. Yet we are dismayed by the crowds of people jostling for tea, snacks, sandwiches, ice cream, and personal space in line. The interior tour is very fine, the white swans are majestic, the history captivating, but I would rather be with the sweaty pilgrims on the North Downs Way or Pilgrim's Way. I feel as though I am queuing up for a rock concert. In fact, Leeds previously hosted Elton John, the Indigo Girls, and Van Morrison events, and this year paying customers can see the Royal Philharmonic, Down for the Count Swing Orchestra, and a fly-over by historic Spitfire warplanes. Okay, if that is your cup of tea.

Leeds does have a somewhat quirky diversion, a dog collar museum displaying canine neckwear from the 15th through the 19th centuries. I enjoy it more than the castle. The Brits do have a thing for dogs—as well as gardens. So many off-leash dogs greet us on the trail that we positively expect them—very, very rare is the lone walker without a canine companion. The trail companion dogs are always well-behaved and nonchalant, never jumping up or harassing us. As with all the sports and games we Americans inherited from the mother country, the love of rural villages, dogs, cats, and horses are more shared passions.

The "special relationship" and all that—one can feel very at home in the UK. I love the States, but I could honestly live in England if my extended family were magically transported here. To be blunt, sometimes I feel that Brits are more humorous, eloquent, literate, humane, gentle, smart, and more charmingly self-deprecating than many of my peers at home. The NHS is much maligned but amazingly effective at delivering health care. Educational standards are very high. The quality of life and happiness are evident. So many partnerships and programs exist to protect the natural environment and combat climate change. Citizens in the UK support their fine and performing arts and are engaged in local concerts, plays, and exhibitions. Nothing against America; it's just not possible to go on a real pilgrimage at home. I feel safe in England, though it is not free of the standard murders, robberies, subway bombings, and burglaries. Unlike at home, I feel there is zero chance of an irate active shooter with an AR-15 at any school, church, or shopping mall in Britain.

Back to the walking, we ascend another steep ridge and find the path undulates between the NDW on the ridge top and the PW lower down, usually along a gravel road. Nearby Hollingbourne village features the Dirty Habit Pub, a modern re-appellation for an old establishment formerly called the King's Head, a darkly appropriate name. After the 17th century English Civil War between parliamentarians and royalists, King James II stayed in this pub's rooms on his way to seek refuge in France. The king wanted to keep his head on, and the French had yet to revolutionize the three estates and guillotine the king, queen, and royalists. During the English Civil War, King James's brother King Charles I was tried, convicted, and beheaded for treason in 1649.

Getting closer to Lenham, we see another ominous sight: a gate at the Summoner's Farm warning of "guard dogs on duty." They look like German Shepherds. All the dogs we have met are friendly, but it is the farm's name that repels us more. In *The Canterbury Tales*, the Summoner is Chaucer's most repulsive character with his face scarred by leprosy. Children are afraid to look at him. His job is to summon offenders to clerical court to pay fines for their sins. Chaucer's Summoner takes bribes, often gets drunk, and utters the Latin *"questio quid juris"* (I question which law applies to your offense) to intimidate his clients. We do not go into this farm and continue on the trail, which bypasses the stout metal gate.

One sight that is strangely interesting is not a church or castle but a factory near Harrietsham called the Marley. We see several long, low buildings, trucks, and warehouses. The Marley was started in 1923 by Owen Asher as the Marley Joinery Works making windows and doors. The company expanded and became famous for its tiles, drainage pipes, gutters, and pitched roofing materials. Many people who are lucky enough to own a home in the UK boast about their Marley roof tiles or drains. The factory is now part of an international corporation called Aliaxis and still makes products locally under the Marley name. The factory is a rare example of formerly great-quality English manufacturers still here and not outsourced overseas. As Bill Bryson opines in *The Road to Little Dribbling*, way back in the 1960s, all the most desired, high quality, and fashionable products came from England. A tiny bit of this heritage is still left with Rolls Royce and Bentley cars, Doc Martens shoes, and Cadbury's chocolates. Okay, I know that Rolls Royce and Bentley cars are now built by German companies.

Most people would not have heard of the Marley factory, but many PBS (Public Broadcasting Service) fans at home would recognize the Lenham Memorial cross. We see it perched high on a hill as we walk into town. Built in 1922, the cross sits high above the village carved into the chalk hillside in a fashion like the Westbury White Horse in Wiltshire or the Long Man of Wilmington, East Sussex.

Like many other memorials, the 200-foot Lenham Cross was constructed by villagers as a tribute to the 42 locals who died in the First World War. It was covered with grass in the Second World War to avoid supplying navigational aid to German warplanes coming over the English Channel from the continent. In a nation of so many historic but largely empty churches, there are still signs of the public embrace of faith such as this. Although filled with disputes and controversies like all churches, the Church of England (or Worldwide Anglican Communion) does create a quasi-common cultural context and a sign of hope amidst the darkness of the 21st century.

Arriving in Lenham, we visit St. Mary's church and meet three gregarious, white-haired ladies who appear to be tourists poking around the sanctuary as we look for the pilgrim's stamp. They are not local and speak with heavy Eastern European accents. We talk of our adventures on the Pilgrim's Way, and the three ladies seem impressed, but we are not out to impress anyone and feel embarrassed. The ladies are accompanied by a fourth person who seems to be a villager. We do not want to ask but it is possible these three are Ukrainian refugees driven out by the Russian invasion and are hosted by the village parish. There is so much visible support for Ukraine in the UK: churches, private houses, benefits, and towns are often fly the blue and yellow flag. Another example of British hospitality, the golden rule, and the Guardian Angels we seem to conjure up.

My favorite sight of the day is not a factory or hill memorial but Brother Percival, who is a wooden statue of a monk on pilgrimage who has decided to rest, going to sleep on a bench underneath a shade tree (above). I sit down beside him and place my hat on his head, commiserating with what he surely felt at this point in the long walk from Winchester to Canterbury. Bro. Percy looks to be a contented, plump Franciscan, smiling with his head resting on his raised right hand. Though tired, he is happy to be on pilgrimage, released temporarily from his dull, cloistered life spent praying and copying manuscripts. The Kent Downs Countryside Partnership and the local parish commissioned the sculptor to create and install the monk here on his bench, right on the Pilgrim's Way. He looks exactly like what many walkers must be feeling if they have come more than 120 miles. I feel an immediate bond with him and enjoy my time in his space.

Chapter 14: Lenham to Wye

Field of the Cloth of Gold

The New Flying Horse Pub in Wye, Kent offers two levels of service demarcated by the size of bell rung

We enjoy a glass of wine and pint of ale to celebrate a day of rest and train rides: cheers!

Last night's dinner in Lenham was splendid—monkfish and prawn curry with potatoes and green vegetables. Who said that British pub food was abysmal? Every time we have lunch or dinner in a pub, we are never disappointed with the quality and variety of food on offer. Each menu is unique, and the chef often has daily specials and interesting dishes with local ingredients.

Our journey is getting close to the end, and I will be glad to go home, yet I will miss English food, people, pubs, walks, dogs, churches, ale, and so much more.

After breakfast, I realize I have carried away the room key from the previous day's B&B at Thurnham—drat! I see a Royal Mail office across the road and go to ship the key back. I have difficulties understanding the clerk, who tries to be helpful with selecting the packaging. I do not know if it is the dense plate glass between us, the clerk's Covid mask, her local accent, or my incipient age-related hearing loss. I have been tested for hearing aids but have not bought them because of the expense and my ongoing state of denial—am I really *that* old? Despite all odds, the key is successfully sent back to its home.

It is raining again today, so we decide to shorten the walk and taxi to Charing so we can see the church and Archbishop's Palace (somewhat in ruins). Charing is only one day's horseback ride from Canterbury (about fifteen miles), and the palace and manor had served as a lodging stop for many archbishops and kings who went back and forth across Southeast England. Leigh Hatts wrote that King Henry VIII stayed here in 1520, just a decade before he was to break with Rome over his desire to marry Anne Boleyn. In a place deeply scripted by history, we find many claims to fame such as a stone referenced by Becket and the block on which John the Baptist was beheaded, a relic supposedly brought from the Holy Land.

The Charing Palace tower dates from the 14th century. Pilgrims to Canterbury during the last hundred years before the Reformation would have entered it or used its keyhole for receiving alms. The plaque above the hole reads, "Alms were handed through the small window below to those in need. Charing Parish treated its poor well." From the looks of it, the poor would not be getting a feast through this narrow slot.

When King Henry VIII came to Charing in 1520, he was on an important diplomatic journey across the English Channel to Balinghem, where he held a summit with King Frances I of France. Henry was traveling with a huge entourage of 5,000 people including his first wife, Catherine of Aragon. Henry wanted to impress Francis, so he needed to bring lots of equipment, tents, retainers, courtiers, cooks, military men, and diplomats.

In the early 16th century, France and Britain were rising powers of Western Europe, both strongly Roman Catholic before the Reformation. The two kings needed to court each other in a political alliance to avoid war and to provide a counterbalance to the Holy Roman Empire, which was a loose alliance of largely Germanic states led by the Hapsburg King Charles V. Henry tried to enlist Francis's assistance in pressuring Pope Clement VII to declare the English king's first marriage illegitimate. Queen Catherine had produced no male offspring. Henry wanted to court Anne Boleyn, so he severed links with Rome and declared himself Supreme Head on Earth of the Church of England in 1534.

The field in Northern France, Pas-de-Calais, where the English and French kings met, came to be called *Camp du Drap d'Or* (Field of the Cloth of Gold). Attempting to outshine each other, Henry and Francis wore their most extravagant clothing and paraded around with their huge entourages. The kings put up fancy royal tents and hosted feasts with music, jousting tournaments, and games. The fabrics used in the royal tents featured so much gold and silk thread that the field where they met in France was renamed. So much golden cloth on one anonymous field!

Because of the continuing rain in Charing town, we decide to shorten the day. We will ride the local train to Wye, a village a short two stops away, which gives us rest and recovery time for the long, final push into Canterbury tomorrow and the complicated transition home ahead. Today's trail is mostly flat, but we still need some rest. Realizing we are near the end and are about to enter Canterbury, I think about my mother again and the recent end of her own journey.

The village Wye turns out to be very beautiful with St. Gregory and St. Martin's Church right across the road from our combination B&B and pub. Inside, a serious-looking church organ repairman labors with his head inserted inside a tall wooden box of organ pipes. We still look around inside to find the stamp without success this time, and to read the placards.

The village name instantly makes me think of Wordsworth's poem "Tintern Abbey," which has a very long complete title: "Lines Composed a Few Miles Above Tintern Abbey, on Revisiting the Banks of the Wye during a Tour, July 13, 1798." Wordsworth wrote it during a walking tour with his sister Dorothy, and said, "No poem of mine was composed under circumstances more pleasant for me to remember than this. I began it upon leaving Tintern, after crossing the Wye, and concluded it just as I was entering Bristol in the evening, after a ramble of four or five days with my notes. Not a line of it was altered, not any part of it written down till I reached Bristol."

For me, Wordsworth's poem defines the Romantic movement; it explains the process of imaginative reconstruction of memory and how affective experience creates meaning. The story also shows how important Wordsworth's walking tours were in his writing process.

The green spaces and graveyards adjacent to the St. Gregory and St. Martin's church in Wye have been allowed to grow wild to serve as pollinator and wildflower habitat. The long grass by gravestones looks messy but seems a good idea for a multi-purpose common space. In America, some states have followed this lead and created "No Mow May" programs to entice people to not cut their lawns in early spring, helping the pollinator insects to thrive.

Many people on long walks or pilgrimage often undertake non-material "work" on their inner state of being. I know that possibility motivated me to arrange this walk to Canterbury. Both Claudia and I are processing and grieving at times. Grief and happiness commingle. We are also celebrating grown children, two healthy grandbabies, imminent retirement, and future travel plans.

Peter Matthiessen's *The Snow Leopard* is the story of another kind of pilgrimage. In 1973, the author traveled with the field biologist George Schaller to the remote mountains of Nepal to study the elusive high-altitude wild cat, which at the time had never been observed *in situ*. Nepal was still exotic, unexplored, and unfamiliar to Westerners before mass tourism and the commercially guided expeditions on Mt. Everest. Matthiessen is looking for the snow leopard, and he is also on a spiritual quest to find an ancient Buddhist shrine in the mountains to quell his inner demons. His real work is internal. He is processing more than wild animal habitats and the physical demands of climbing in the Himalayas. The author lost his wife to cancer the previous year, and he left behind an eight-year-old son who is afraid of losing both parents. As a Buddhist, Matthiessen is trying to use his faith to achieve some degree of solace or psychological composure. He is trying to detach himself from desire. That must be harder than going into a nice English pub and not ordering fish and chips with a pint of local bitter.

A book by Timothy Egan, similar in some ways, is called *A Pilgrimage to Eternity*. Egan describes the beginning of his pilgrimage to Canterbury, then makes his way on to the continent and the Via Francigena, an ancient route that resumes after crossing the English Channel before winding through France, Switzerland, and Italy, ending in Rome at Vatican City. At over 1,000 miles, the trail goes through a variety of farmland, cities, and mountains. Egan knew he could not walk the entire length and used efficient European trains periodically. Once again, his purpose is three-fold: 1) he wants to do the difficult physical task of walking across a big part of Europe; 2) his internal work is to figure out a way to rekindle some element of his Catholic faith lost in years of scandals and betrayals, and 3) the author also is coming to terms with the impending death of his sister-in-law due to cancer.

As for my mother's pilgrimage of life, she lived a long and productive, happy life, but not without periods of darkness. One story never discussed openly in my family was my mother's time in a psychiatric hospital. When I was three years old, she attempted suicide and was kept away from home for several weeks under doctor's orders. She underwent electroshock therapy, which was controversial, then and is still now. No one ever discussed this. I learned about it through oblique innuendos and allusions—until we went through her papers.

Two years ago, Claudia and I had to de-clutter and remove 50+ years of possessions from her house when she broke her hip, had emergency surgery, and needed to move into assisted living. In only one week's time at the beginning of the COVID-19 pandemic, we emptied out rooms and made uncounted trips to charity shops, libraries, recycling centers, and the city garbage dump – whatever we could find open during the pandemic closures. We needed to clean out the house and get it ready for sale because we lived far away and were there on spring break from school. The realtor had lined up showings with prospective buyers. Working frantically and without much sleep, I tried to keep any bits of paper that looked like official records such as her marriage certificate, Social Security and Medicare documents, and financials. Among her papers deep in the back of a closet, I found a series of handwritten letters.

Sixty years later, it is impossible to know the complete story. The Michigan hospital was long ago demolished, and medical records from the early 1960s are gone. The letters are heart-rending and pleading love notes written by my father and my sister to my mother. My sister is four years older than I am, and back then, she helped to take care of two babies with the assistance of a hired housemaid. Most of the letters use the salutation "Dearest Sarah" and are signed, "Always loving you, Dad."

I am surprised the letters survived.

I found only one short letter written by my mother to my father and a couple notes from my sister. All the letters are written by my father except for this one. My mother's letter is the most remarkable written document she left behind. I quote her letter in its entirety in my attempt to understand her state of mind:

> Dearest Sam,
>
> I am looking forward to seeing you on Thursday. I will be able to go out from 2:00 until 4:00 PM. Maybe we could go to a restaurant and have coffee. Glad to hear that you are getting a new suit of clothes. I know you needed one badly. I wrote to my mother and enclosed the check you sent. Thanks very much.
>
> Yesterday, I had a conference with Dr. Everett. He thinks that something was bothering me subconsciously that caused me to take the overdose of tranquillizers and he wants me to try to find out what it is. I imagine he will talk to you when you come on Thursday. I asked him if I can go home soon, but he will not

give me any idea about how soon he will release me. I miss you and the children so much it hurts. I surely hope he will let me go home soon. However, I would not want to give you any trouble. I cannot understand why I behaved so badly. I hope that I am cured now. Even though the patients are well taken care of here, it is rather irritating to be told what to do, when to be locked in and out, and not allowed to go anywhere without a nurse!

I want you to remember that I love you very much. Give my love to Margie, Jon, and Nick. Could you bring a picture of the boys? I can't even remember what they look like.

Lots of love, Sarah

I cannot fully grasp or understand the situation she faced living in a small Midwestern town in the 1950s and 1960s. I am struck by my mother's directness, confession, fear of being inconvenient, lack of introspective analysis, dislike of rules, and her thwarted attempt to express feelings. In the letter, she sounds like she wants to leave the hospital and come home, but she is unable or unwilling to state the exact reason behind her actions.

My father taught at the local college, and my mother adored him, but he was a difficult person, probably an undiagnosed autistic with depressive tendencies. He rarely spoke to me or my mother and was easily upset by social gatherings, interruptions of routine, and loud noises. The marriage to my mother was his second marriage and her first; he was 45 and she was 23 when they wed in 1950, so it was a classic May/ December scenario.

By any objective measure, my father Samuel L. Thorndike was successful: two marriages, five children, graduate of America's most prestigious universities, studied at Cambridge, worked at MIT in the 1940s in the radiation lab, taught navigation to Navy cadets in the V-5 and V-12 programs during the Second World War, taught math, physics, and astronomy at several colleges, and played viola in the college orchestra. He was a good provider, but he didn't talk much to begin with, and he never talked with me about his life. He was patient with me and helped me with my algebra and trigonometry in high school, but I was troubled as a youth and needed guidance he was unable to provide.

I inherited some of my father's social anxieties and autistic tendencies. I do not blame my father or my mother for anything. They gave me life. They provided me with a loving home to the best of their abilities.

Most troubling to me is my mother's suicide attempt—what would have prompted that, I can only guess. She had three young children to care for in a small Michigan town far away from her family in South Carolina. She probably received little help from my father given his age, inclinations, and the *Leave it to Beaver* culture of the time.

Processing the fact of my mother's hospitalization and attempt at taking her own life is not the purpose of our pilgrimage to Canterbury, but it is also unavoidable, lodged in my memory like an abscessed tooth that needs to be x-rayed and pulled. I think about her every day. What prompts someone to become so despondent and hopeless that she no longer wants to live? How close did I come to being motherless at three years old? Unanswerable, I know. There are probably countless factors, and I could never understand another person's mind. I take some comfort in my mother's long life and her continued community involvement. She had many friends and was generally happy up to her death at age 95. She never gave in to the darkness, and she lived a long life. She never attempted suicide again. She always kept Dylan Thomas's poem "Do Not

Go Gentle into That Good Night" on her refrigerator with its refrain:

> And you, my father, there on the sad height,
> Curse, bless, me now with your fierce tears, I pray.
> Do not go gentle into that good night.
> Rage, rage against the dying of the light.

Was it rage, despair, depression, bi-polar disorder? I will never know. As the cliché says, my mother took some secrets with her to the grave, and this was not the only one. She might have been one of my father's students in college; perhaps he was still married to his first wife. She never mentioned how the two of them met.

For me, this brings in the purpose of faith. This is the purpose of pilgrimage, in part, to deepen my understanding of self, God, and the human social animal. I am not embarrassed to say I believe in God, Jesus, and the Holy Spirit. I know this does not change anything materially but underlines immeasurable qualities of love, forgiveness, benevolence, gratitude, kindness, beneficence. A mother's love for her baby—who could quantify that? The fact of living for something, someone, or devoted to a purpose beyond the self, showing compassion to the stranger—this is the purpose of any religion—lessons that never change, that need to be continually studied and re-learned, that are woefully underdeveloped in my character and lacking in the world.

I do not believe in magic, and I do trust the cold, dispassionate world of facts, logic, empiricism, and science. My mother did not believe in God, but I believe I will meet her again in another plane of existence, in another dimension of the time-space continuum, in the mysterious realm of clouds, rain, and the stars, in the Holy City of Jerusalem that does and does not exist anywhere in the world, in the Field of the Cloth of Gold.

In some ways, my mother lived a difficult life, and she fought the good fight when depression or other psychological factors prompted her to want to die. She did not believe in God, but she loved the gods of house cats, compassion, gardens, kindness, flowers, golf, wild birds, the Indigo Bunting, Mozart, Bach, and Beethoven, European travel, Charleston and Boston, the MET opera radio broadcasts, cappuccino, church choir, bridge club, summer barbeques, Christmas cookies, geraniums and begonias, beachside vacations, Verdi and Puccini, Thanksgiving feasts, deli sandwiches, libraries and books, children, Michigan strawberries, grandchildren, church grounds cleanup day, Lady's Hospital Auxiliary, corn on the cob, education for women, education for grandchildren, caramel macchiato, house cleaners, hot dogs, Pizza Sam's Special, Michigan State Parks, and the Appalachian Trail.

She loved the God of love.

Now back to the Canterbury pilgrimage—we see water dripping in the corner of the beautiful, old St. Gregory and St. Martin Church in Wye that is near our B&B. Despite the leaky roof, this space is lovely and is loved. Thank God the church is still here and has not been replaced by an electronics store or car park. The church organ technician continues his drilling, oblivious to us, tearing out the wall, tunneling, and installing new pipes for future concerts and services.

Despite the dripping water and need for roof repair, we see abundant evidence of human activity and investment here in Wye and in so many small parish churches of rural England. We only found one church that was completely shut down on the entire Pilgrim's Way, and it was still open for casual visitors who wanted to know about a Spitfire airplane that crashed nearby in the 1940s. It is obvious people still love these ancient churches, comfortable in their old bones and faded majesty. Remodeling constantly happens when a church goes back to the time of St. Thomas à Becket, St. Swithun, and St. William of Perth. We see posters and adverts for children's programs, raising money for charities, the crisis in Ukraine, elder care, Bible study, hospital volunteers, community gardens, choir concerts, environmental stewardship, working with the homeless, the handicapped, the abused and abandoned, the poor—eternal, unfinished missions. As long as there are people on this earth.

Still lost in such musings, we walk back to the homely house at the end of the world, the New Flying Horse hotel and pub near the River Wye, which Wordsworth referenced in "Tintern Abbey" (although I learn *that* river Wye is in Wales, not Kent). The rooms are converted horse stables newly decorated with fresh paint and tasteful wall sconces. Walking down the lane from the church, we notice an elderly gent with a cane slowly making his way to the same pub. He is wearing a frizzled, dark green sweater and has a gray beard and woolen cap. It is almost dinner time, so we sit in the pub and have a drink first. The old man sits by himself just behind the door and says a few pleasant words to the barkeep and to other visitors. This seems like a routine for him, perhaps his only social outing every day. This is what matters in the world—to have family near or to be able to visit the local pub in absence of a family.

Chelsea Pensioner, a veteran of
the British Army living in Royal
Hospital, London

Overgrown greenery around a
disused cottage at the New
Flying Horse, Wye

Just behind the New Flying Horse, a sight that seems so English—a decrepit Chelsea Pensioner sign hangs above an overgrown cottage (an accidental but appropriate reference to the
man in the pub). The Royal Hospital, Chelsea, is a retirement
and nursing home for British Army veterans in a fashionable
London neighborhood (which was probably not fashionable in
the 17th century when it was built). I have no idea why the sign
would be in this village except as an attractive ornament. Moss
and wild grasses grow above the sign frame. The pensioner is
wearing the classic scarlet coat and tricorne hat used by the
Brits in the American Revolutionary War. His expression says
it all—resigned, stoic, patriotic, devoted to king and country.
We honor our veterans in the States in different ways, but we
do not see them in ceremonial wear in public places like you

do sometimes here at concerts or at the Wimbledon tennis tournament.

Next to the sign is a cottage with overgrown greenery and thatched roof, the trees and shrubs literally growing out of the building, long disused. The cottage was originally the owner's house and now sits without a purpose—so much like England, too beautiful to replace and too obsolete to renovate but continuing its own merry way to the happy place of being overtaken by nature.

Chapter 15: Wye to Canterbury

Bob Up and Down and the Meddlesome Priest

Canterbury Cathedral was founded in 597 CE by St. Augustine, who was sent by Pope Gregory as a missionary to Kent to convert the pagan Celts

Site of Thomas à Becket's martyrdom in the Cathedral, commemorated by Giles Blomfield's sculpture and altar representing the knights' four swords that killed him on 29 December 1170 CE

I have always enjoyed long walks and have a history of pursuing various kinds of trails and gravel paths. When I was in high school, it seemed a good idea to backpack across the upper half of my home state of Michigan during spring break (still winter in Upper Michigan). I convinced a friend to go with me, and we marched for a week through heavy snow which was usually still frozen. We could make good time by walking on top of the thick snow crust unless the temperature rose above freezing, which caused us to fall down up to our knees in snowbanks.

One summer while in college, I worked at a rustic hotel in Isle Royale National Park. My bellhop and kitchen gopher job allowed me weekends off to do long solo overnight hikes across the remote island in the middle of cold, vast Lake Superior. I also did multi-day backpacking trips in Michigan, Wisconsin, and on the Appalachian Trail on the Tennessee and North Carolina border.

I always wanted to walk a long European pilgrimage, and luckily, Claudia was happy to join me. So, we walked the Pilgrim's Way.

Besides Chaucer's *Canterbury Tales*, a book by Hilaire Belloc inspired me to hike the Pilgrim's Way: *The Old Road* (1904). The opening passage below is stylistically like something written by Joseph Campbell, the beloved Sarah Lawrence professor of comparative mythology who starred in his own PBS series, interviewed by Bill Moyers. Belloc is not so concerned with objective evidence for the PW at first; he wants to find deeper meaning, broader resonance, evidence for the "most original of the spells we inherit from the earliest pioneers of our race." I love that phrase, and Belloc's opening paragraphs, which seem to come directly from Jungian dream consciousness:

> There are primal things which move us. Fire has the character of a free companion that has travelled with us from the first exile; only to see a fire, whether he need it or no, comforts every man. Again, to hear two

voices outside at night after a silence, even in crowded cities, transforms the mind...we craved these things—the camp, the refuge, the sentinels in the dark, the hearth—before we made them; they are part of our human manner, and when this civilization has perished, they will reappear. *Of these primal things the least obvious but the most important is The Road*...Men, indeed, whose pleasure it is perpetually to explore even their own country on foot, and to whom its every phase of climate is delightful, receive, somewhat tardily, the spirit of The Road. They feel a meaning in it; it grows to suggest the towns upon it, it explains its own vagaries, and it gives a unity to all that has arisen along its way... [it is] the most original of the spells which we inherit from the earliest pioneers of our race (my italics; 3).

We are walking from Wye to Canterbury. This is to be our last day hiking, and I do not know if we are channeling the primal spirit of the road, but we are happy and sad to be nearing the conclusion. I do not know if we will ever return here. Like so many things in life, the end can be anti-climactic; happiness is developed in the preparation and the performance of the journey itself, not the arrival and end. When this pilgrimage ends, what do we do next? Keep walking to Rome? We have unfinished business at home, friends to meet, tasks to complete, fresh strawberries to eat, grandchildren to greet. We have promises to keep, and miles to go before we sleep in Canterbury at the Millers Arms hotel.

How many things in life, if we were to know at the time that we will never do them again, would we do with greater sensitivity, appreciation, grace, and love?

Part of me wants to keep my "pilgrim self" alive and not return to normal life back home. Just cross the English Channel at Dover and keep walking through France. At home, I know

I will have to do the regular chores, sweep the floor, file the taxes, fix the broken cabinet, pick up doggy poop, mow the lawn. I am always impatient and quick to complete things, but I know I will be sad at the conclusion of this long walk. The road is a primal attraction as Belloc wrote, and although filled with hardship and disappointment, it is also addictive. Life is a road, a journey. Being a pilgrim is both easier and harder than my normal day-to-day life. People are kind to strangers who are pilgrims, and I have no responsibility in Britain except to make it to the next village or church.

The day after today, we will be sitting on the train to St. Pancras station and then to Heathrow, which brings the flight home. Because we took the train yesterday to Wye, we are backtracking to Boughton Lees and the infamous King's Wood, where ancient pilgrims were forced to band together to evade robbers who camped out there due to its proximity to the end point and famous Becket shrine attracting all manner of pilgrims, paupers, and kings. We do not expect to see any robbers or kings. Today's robbers have all but disappeared into the Internet to develop elaborate cell phone and computer hacking scams. Apparently, if the weather is clear, walkers can see the distant spire of Canterbury Cathedral at the end of King's Wood, rising majestically about seven miles away like a faerie castle in the misty clouds of a Miyazaki anime film. To-day there are some clouds, so we do not see the cathedral. Yet. We are so close!

Also close by on our right is Godmersham Park with a two-story Palladian mansion built in the 18th century. The house features a long, stately grass walking path entrance. It was once owned by Jane Austen's brother Edward. Biographers be-lieve Jane Austen wrote parts of her novels *Pride and Prejudice, Emma,* and *Mansfield Park* here as well as at Chawton. I had no idea Godmersham was this close to Canterbury. In 2017 when the new British £10 note made its debut to commemorate 200 years after her death, the bill featured Jane Austen's portrait with Godmersham in the background.

The trail today, though not as long as some previous days' walks, does have some steep ascents coming out of the village of Chilham. The trail passes through more interesting historical place names such as Old Wives Lees, No Man's Orchard, Bigbury Iron Age Fort, and Harbledown. Sitting on a bench for a rest, we see many large vineyards and fruit tree farms that seem to stretch for miles. Agricultural workers tend to live in either Chilham or Old Wives Lees instead of more expensive and touristy Canterbury.

Old Wives Lees was known as "Old Wyves Lease" in the 17th century, so the village may have been a refuge for widows of husbands employed in Chilham village. Like so many English names, there is a long backstory, many variations, and different etymological theories to delight amateur antiquarians and philologists. According to Saunders, there is another explanation for the unusual village name: it could be a corruption of Oldwood's Lees, a reference to John Oldwood, a 15th century squire who lived here. "Lees" could be a variation of "leas" or meadows, so the village name possibly means John Oldwood's meadows.

After the ascent into Old Wives Lees, we see some horse pastures with brown and white ponies sauntering nearby. We cross through the strangely named "No Man's Orchard Nature Reserve," which has many varieties of blossoming apple trees, long wild grasses, and a huge wooden snake sculpture partially hidden beneath the grass. I seize the opportunity to tease Claudia about seeing a big snake, as she likes snakes even less than I. "No Man's Orchard" looks like a crazy old hippie's farm, and I expect to see Grateful Dead t-shirts and posters. Or is this the biblical Garden of Eden with the devil hidden behind the apple tree in the grass? Walking through the wild orchard with a light rain falling, we seem to be returning to the elven haven of Lothlórien in Tolkien's Middle Earth, so close to civilization yet surrounded by natural wonders. Why would any land in England be called "No Man's" when there is hardly any free, open land in this small island nation?

According to the Kentish Stour Countryside Partnership website, the orchard was acquired in 1996 and called "No Man's Orchard" because it straddles two Canterbury parishes. Church administrators could not decide which parish governed it (if there were any Church of England trees or animals). When the owner was ready to sell, the Partnership bought the orchard for a wildlife habitat that is friendly to birds, insects, wildflowers, reptiles, lichens, and mosses. "No Man's Orchard" includes Bramley Apple trees planted in the 1940s, still growing big and strong. It was the first orchard in Britain designated as a Local Wildlife Site and Nature Reserve and was protected from any development. The apples keep growing on their own; I suspect that neighboring villagers keep their eyes on the trees.

I am impressed with England's ability to rein in suburban sprawl and retain the green space around most cities. Everywhere we go, we see signs of people and organizations that care deeply about protecting land from development. Like all things, this does not come without a cost, and one problem created is a lack of housing.

Next, we see Bigbury Iron Age Fort, which seems nothing more than a huge, raised dirt rectangle surrounded by more trees. Archeologists have found enough metal artifacts here to think ancient Britons built it, then retreated upon the arrival of Julius Caesar, who landed with his legionnaires at the coastal town of Deal in 54 BCE. I can imagine the comparatively primitive, goat-skin covered Britons running for the hills when they saw the invading armies, imposing ships, and shining armor of Caesar's troops.

Caesar famously wrote "*Gallia est omnis divisa in partes tres*" ("All Gaul is divided into three parts") as the opening sentence in his eyewitness account, *The Conquest of Gaul*, published between 58 and 49 BCE. The "Gaul" which Caesar divided up so neatly was ambiguous geographically but probably included most of France and parts of Belgium, Germany, and Switzerland. The fact that Caesar made it to Britain is testimony to his world-conquering ego. The opening sentence is the ultimate statement of hubris. In the end, Caesar abandoned his attempt to conquer Britain and returned to Rome to start a civil war, to declare himself *dictator perpetuo* ("dictator for life"), and to be assassinated by a group of rogue senators on 15 March 44 BCE, "the Ides of March." Because of Shakespeare and Plutarch, we will never overlook that date!

Harbledown is just outside of Canterbury and practically connected with it, and it has an even more interesting name etymology. In Chaucer's *Canterbury Tales*, towards the end of the book, the host attempts to wake the Cook to tell his story—it is his turn. The Cook is too drunk to be coherent, so the Manciple jumps in with a preface to his own story:

Do you not know where there is a little town
That is called by all about "Bob-Up-and-Down"
Under the Blean, down Canterbury Way?

Harbledown is the last stop for Chaucer's pilgrims. The name sounds very much like the Manciple's name for it, which refers to a hill before the entrance to the village. Pilgrims would "bob up and down" as they ascended and descended into Canterbury. Harbledown is also the home of St. Dunstan's Church, the last one before the awe-inspiring spires of Canterbury, the home of the archbishop.

Another theory for the town's name refers to 12 July 1174, when King Henry came here to do his penance four years after the murder of Becket. The name of Harbledown could reference being "hobbled"—not having a horse or walking barefoot to the Becket shrine, as was done by the king.

Historians believe that Becket had undergone a religious awakening after his appointment as Archbishop in 1162 CE. He started to take his religious calling seriously. Studying the Bible and daily prayer convinced him to do more work serving the poor. Previously in the job of Chancellor, Becket had become a close friend of King Henry II. They became entangled in a dispute about the archbishop's powers over secular courts and government. The king wanted Becket and the church to defer to him. He also wanted to divorce a wife who did not produce a male heir. Becket is venerated by both the Catholic and Anglican faith communities because he refused to compromise the integrity of the church in the face of rising royal powers. After Becket's death, pilgrims flocked to his shrine for what St. Thomas represented—an idea more powerful than armies. Pope Alexander III proclaimed Becket a saint in 1173, just three years after his death.

Some pilgrims take off their shoes and walk the last half mile. Claudia and I do not remove our shoes as we walk into Canterbury town and make our way to the Cathedral. The high street is lined with all the standard chain stores, boutique shops, restaurants, gambling outlets, vape and cell phone stores, pubs, and banks a person could want. It is not a solemn stroll through verdant barley fields, forests, or the North Downs of Kent. Worldly, fleshly temptations were also abundant in Chaucer's day and another reason people wanted to walk there. Since St. Thomas attracted pilgrims, local businesses would want to capitalize on the foot traffic and potential customers walking past their doors. I always patronize a great Oxfam used bookstore on my visits to Canterbury, and I'm sure that same store would struggle if removed from pilgrim traffic.

Our entry into the Cathedral itself is anti-climactic. As we approach the gateway, a cathedral staff person wearing a blue vest looks us over.

"Hello, we are pilgrims who've walked from Winchester."

"Well, so you have! Congratulations, right this way, I will get you your stamp and you can enter the cathedral."

This is the extent of our reception. I am not expecting brass band salutes, a medallion from the archbishop, or a flyover by the RAF. We are too exhausted to request a ritual blessing and prayer with a staff priest like we had enjoyed in Winchester. We want to look around the cathedral a bit and walk back to our hotel to have a beer, dinner, and take a shower. We need to get ready for a long train trip and flight the next day. After dinner, we return to hear the evensong service, which is the best kind of reception we can hope for.

I am struck by the enormity and ethereal beauty of the cathedral, but I am more interested in what St. Thomas was like as a person. *The Pillars of the Earth* is a work of fiction by Ken Follett, but I love the author's imaginary recreation of Thomas:

> Philip [the monk who built Kingsbridge Cathedral] looked up to see Archbishop Thomas of Canterbury.
>
> He was immediately aware of being in the presence of a remarkable man. Thomas was tall, slender, and exceptionally handsome, with a wide forehead, bright eyes, fair skin, and dark hair. He was about 10 years younger than Phillip, around 50 or 51. Despite his misfortunes, he had a lively, cheerful expression. He was, Phillip saw instantly, a very attractive man, and this partly explained his remarkable rise from humble beginnings. Phillip knelt and kissed his hand.
>
> Thomas said, "I am so glad to make your acquaintance! I've always wanted to visit Knightsbridge—I've

heard so much about your priory and the marvelous new cathedral" (936).

King Henry II decided Becket's murder was God's punishment for what had happened, the "unintentional" execution order. When the king supposedly said, "Who will rid me of this meddlesome priest," the knights took it literally. They entered the cathedral through a side door while Thomas was at prayer. One knight hacked off the top of Thomas's skull, cut his arm deeply and let it bleed out, and another lifted his head and slashed Thomas's throat. His brains and blood spilled out on the sacred cathedral floor. Legend says that monks quickly tried to recover the blood, brain fragments, and body.

Four years later at St. Dunstan's church in the last half-mile of his penitential pilgrimage, King Henry II got off his horse, removed his royal gown, put on a hair shirt and cloak, and walked barefoot the rest of the way to the cathedral. He had become a common sinner. He may have uttered the Jesus Prayer: "Lord Jesus Christ, son of God, have mercy on me, a sinner." In that moment, he was no longer the king but a broken, fallen man who had seriously miscalculated the intentions of his clerical advisor and friend. After he dismounted and walked barefoot, King Henry allowed himself to be whipped by bishops while he prayed for forgiveness.

St. Thomas's defiance of the king's power changed nothing materially, but like all powerful ideas, it moved mountains without coercion or duress because it was intrinsic, on the side of justice, in the hearts of people. Gandhi's "March to the Sea" in 1930 changed nothing about the power of the British colonial government in India. Martin Luther King Jr.'s "March on Washington" and famous speech at the Lincoln Memorial changed little about endemic racism in America in 1963. But these non-material acts changed everything. In her book *Scarred by Struggle, Transformed by Hope,* the Catholic writer

Sr. Joan Chittister wrote what could be the ideal send-off paragraph for pilgrims: "Hope is not a denial of reality. . . Hope is a series of small actions that transform darkness into light. It is putting one foot in front of the other when we can find no reason to do so at all."

The Martyrdom (the site of Thomas's execution) is located on the left inside the cathedral, between the Chapter House and the Quire. The Quire features dark brown choir stalls installed by the Victorians and a huge brass eagle lectern holding the Bible, standing in front of the high altar in the center of the cathedral. The Pilgrim's Way leads to the left of the Quire and down a small set of stairs to the Martyrdom, where the four knights sent by King Henry II on 29 December 1170 killed him. I imagine the millions of pilgrims whose feet have touched these stones. For a moment, we sit on the steps of the Martyrdom, the end point of the Pilgrim's Way, which begins in Winchester Cathedral at St. Swithun's shrine. The path was abolished by King Henry VIII during the Reformation, but now it is revitalized. The Pilgrim's Way still moves common people like us to walk a long distance to experience the glories of rural Britain, to feel a deep weariness, to contemplate mortality and celebrate God's blessings, and to follow the primal attraction of the road, walking an ancient pathway that was for a time the most famous footpath in Western Europe.

Postscript

Climbing a wooden stile outside
of Canterbury, almost there

The journey of a lifetime completed with my beloved life partner in a green and pleasant land

On 15 July, we placed my mother's cremated remains in the columbarium (burial ground for ashes) at First Presbyterian Church, Alma, Michigan, where she had been a member for over 50 years. It was St. Swithun's Day, and a light rain fell as we kneeled over the hole in the ground, surrounded by flowers in a walled garden adjacent to the narthex and sanctuary. Church elders held umbrellas over our heads. Some of us wept silently. The pastor read a eulogy and placed my mother's ashes in the ground. We took turns scooping soil from a bucket and pouring it into the square hole.

Rain kept falling in the days after 15 July in America, *and* Britain endured a dry spell and record heat wave—so Swithun's prognostication was correct on both continents. The church columbarium and nearby town cemetery hold the ashes of my brother, who died at an early age, and my father, who taught math and physics for many years at Alma College. My mother dearly loved this place in the rural Midwest—a river town with history and a scenic 19th century downtown complete with opera house and surrounded by corn fields, golf courses, and miles of open space once occupied by bygone industrial giants. Although she was not religious in a traditional sense, my mother rests on church ground. It is sweet and fitting for this church columbarium to be her place of final rest, the end of the road for her. She is surrounded by the flower gardens that she herself loved and tended for so many years. Alma, Michigan, and Alma College will always be sacred ground, a green and pleasant land in my imagination, a small town where people are decent, humble, hardworking, tolerant, and forgiving.

I thought about the basic elements of life as we put my mother's ashes in the ground. Many religious traditions bring ashes and earth into understanding the end of life. In the traditional Ash Wednesday service at the beginning of Lent, the priest or pastor smudges the foreheads of worshippers saying, "From dust you came, and to dust you shall return." Nothing could be more literal nor a more universal metaphor for the path of life, the road from beginning to end. In the *Book of Common Prayer*, a priest uses this phrase during a funeral: "We therefore commit this body to the ground, earth to earth, ashes to ashes, dust to dust; in sure and certain hope of the Resurrection to eternal life." We returned my mother to the ashes and dust of the ground at the church in Michigan.

When I returned home over the years, I was always taken back to 1970s culture because that decade was formative for me, like a soundtrack to my high school years. In her 1970 pop song "Woodstock," Joni Mitchell, wrote about the road and returning to the earth in a different way, using religious overtones and the journey metaphor:

> I came upon a child of God
> He was walking along the road
> When I asked him, where are you going?
> This he told me
> I'm going down to Yasgur's farm
> Think I'll join a rock and roll band
> I'll camp out on the land
> I'll try and set my soul free
>
> We are stardust, we are golden
> And we've got to get ourselves back to the garden

According to physicists, Joni Mitchell was writing scientific fact as well as poetic phrases in her song when she penned, "We are stardust." The Big Bang creation theory claims that every element on earth was forged in the heart of a massive star. The heaviest elements including gold, lead and uranium were produced in a supernova explosion during the cataclysmic end of this huge star's life, creating planet Earth and all stars and planets in the galaxy. We are thus formed of celestial elements, and we all return to the place of our birth. "We've got to get ourselves back to the garden," in Joni Mitchell's words (sung by Stephen Stills in the best-known version), and my mother has just done that literally because she is near the church garden she tended.

My mother was a proud and independent person, often prickly and unbending in her demands. She was a child of the

Great Depression who worked her way through a college education when that was very unusual for women raised in the early 20th century in the Deep South. She did not suffer fools gladly. She believed in work, education, and family. But at the end of her life, she could not get out of bed. Her legs became fragile sticks lacking muscle tissue, and her body withered down to a desiccated sack of bones covered by loose, crepe-papery skin. She needed daily care and spoon feeding, hardly drinking or eating anything, a ghost of her former virulent self.

We ended our pilgrimage to Canterbury before we returned my mother's ashes to the earth, inside the church columbarium. I know my mother's unorthodoxy presents some degree of dissonance with accepted church dogma, and it does not bother me if we remain open to the many possibilities of an afterlife through the Resurrection, metaphor, family memory, faith community, or spiritual existence. In the end we free our souls in the best way. Perhaps more transcendent is the realization that one life began, nurtured a family, grew in love, and ended. My mother expressed her love for her family, and I knew we existed in that space; we were loved and felt comforted and acknowledged. We mattered. I remember the words of Confucius and answer his question with a resounding yes: "A child has lived for three years before he leaves his mother's arms...did you not receive three years' love from your parents?"

So today, at the end of the journey, we hope for another chance to experience transcendent love, to see paradise or England again and what it may represent. Though a modern nation with all attendant problems, England for us is also a land of enchantment, a place where we can all hope and long to return one day to this "scepter'd isle...this other Eden, demi-paradise, /This fortress built by Nature for herself...

This precious stone set in the silver sea,
Which serves it in the office of a wall,
Or as a moat defensive to a house,
Against the envy of less happier lands,
This blessed plot, this earth, this realm, this England.

References

Austen, Jane, *Emma* (London: John Murray, 1815).

Austen, Jane, *Pride and Prejudice* (London: Thomas Egerton, 1813).

Austen, Jane, *Mansfield Park* (London: Thomas Egerton, 1814).

Austen, Jane, *Sense and Sensibility* (London: Thomas Egerton, 1811).

Barrie, J. M., *Quality Street: A Comedy* (New York: Charles Scribner's Sons, 1923).

Belloc, Hilaire, *The Old Road*, (London: A. Constable, 1904).

Blake, William, *Milton: A Poem in Two Books* (London, 1804-1811).

Bloom, Harold, *The Anxiety of Influence: A Theory of Poetry*, 2nd ed (Oxford: Oxford University Press, 1997).

Bly, Robert, *Iron John: A Book About Men* (Boston: Addison-Wesley, 1990)

Bright, Derek, *The Pilgrims' Way: Fact and Fiction of an Ancient Trackway* (Stroud, Gloucestershire: History Press, 2011).

Brontë, Charlotte, *Jane Eyre*, (London: Smith, Elder, and Co., 1847).

Bryson, Bill, *The Road to Little Dribbling: Adventures of an American in Britain* (New York: Doubleday, 2015)

The Catholic Encyclopedia (New York: Robert Appleton Company, 1912).

Chaucer, Geoffrey, *The Canterbury Tales*, trans. Nevill Coghill (London: Penguin Books, 1951).

Chittister, Joan, *Scarred by Struggle, Transformed by Hope* (Grand Rapids: Eerdman's, 2005).

Dickens, Charles, *Great Expectations* (London: Chapman and Hall, 1861)

Dickens, Charles, *The Pickwick Papers* (London: Chapman and Hall, 1837).

Dickens, Charles, *The Mystery of Edwin Drood* (London: Chapman and Hall, 1870)

Egan, Timothy, *A Pilgrimage to Eternity* (New York: Viking, 2019).

Follett, Ken, *The Pillars of the Earth* (New York: Penguin Books, 1989).

Hatts, Leigh, *Walking The Pilgrims' Way To Canterbury from Winchester and London* (Kendal, Cumbria: Cicerone, 2017)

Huxley, Aldous. *Brave New World* (London: Chatto and Windus, 1932).

Keagan, John, *The First World War* (New York: Alfred A. Knopf, 1999).

Larson, Erik, *The Splendid and the Vile: A Saga of Churchill, Family, and Defiance During the Blitz* (New York: Crown, 2020.

Lewis, C. S., *The Four Loves* (London: Geoffrey Bles, 1960).

Macfarlane, Robert, *The Old Ways: A Journey On Foot* (New York: Penguin Books, 2012).

Macintyre, Ben, *A Spy Among Friends: Kim Philby and the Great Betrayal* (New York:
Crown Publishers, 2014).

Matthiessen, Peter, *The Snow Leopard* (New York: Viking Press, 1978),

Ravensdale, Jack, *In the Steps of Chaucer's Pilgrims: From Southwark to Canterbury from the Air and on Foot* (London: Guild Publishing, 1989)

Rosen, Jody, *Two Wheels Good: The History and Mystery of the Bicycle* (New York: Penguin Random House, 2022).

Saunders, Colin, *North Downs Way* (London: Aurum Press, 2016).

Shelley, Percy Bysshe, *Adonais* (London: Charles Ollier, 1821).

Schumacher, E. F., *Small is Beautiful: Economics as if People Mattered* (London: Blond and Briggs, 1973).

Tolkien, J. R. R., *The Fellowship of the Ring* (London: Allen and Unwin, 1954).

Tolkien, J. R. R., *The Two Towers* (London: Allen and Unwin, 1954).

Tolkien, J. R. R., *The Return of the King* (London: Allen and Unwin, 1955).

Vonnegut, Kurt, *Slaughterhouse-Five, or, The Children's Crusade: A Duty-Dance with Death* (New York: Delacorte, 1969).

Wordsworth, William, *Lyrical Ballads, with A Few Other Poems* (London: A. Arch, 1798).

Acknowledgements

Acknowledgments

We are grateful for the assistance we received from many people in the UK and in the United States, including Colin Duriez in Oxford, who kindly gave us a ride and talked about his research on Dorothy L. Sayers, C. S. Lewis, and J. R. R. Tolkien. The C. S. Lewis Study Centre in Headington run by Tyson Rallens, Warden provided a welcome respite for reading and study away from the throngs of tourists who crowded every street in Oxford. I appreciate the support I received from the C. S. Lewis Foundation of Redlands, California and its president, Steven Elmore. Staying at the Kilns and sitting in Lewis's living room to read were a lifelong dream of mine. Elisabeth and her husband Sean provided another perfect place to stay in Headington, and they were very helpful with printing, scanning, and sending official documents home. The staff of the Weston Special Collections at the Bodleian Library in Oxford and the C. S. Lewis Archive were patient answering questions from a confused American researcher. Mandy and Jack Bright were excellent walking tour providers who communicated with us along the way and helped us negotiate challenges and changes in our itinerary. The Rev. Canon Dr. Roland Reims gave us a warm welcome to Winchester Cathedral.

In Michigan, my friends William Palmer and Rick Amidon gave me a lot of support and helpful ideas about research and writing. In Nashville, we were encouraged by many friends and colleagues who showed much interest in our hiking and writing project: Maggie Monteverde, who hosted the Belmont group in London for many years, Doug Murray, extraordinary musician and Anglophile who found a used book for me in Grantham and an excellent Irish fiddle instructor for me in Nashville. Belmont professors Annette Sisson, Jimmy Davis, and Beth Ritter-Conn all influenced this project in many ways. Marcia McDonald was my first mentor and supported my interests in overseas travel and research for years. Robbie and Mike Pinter were great friends and colleagues supportive of my sabbatical idea. Belmont University generously awarded me a sabbatical to study and travel in England, and I appreciate the support of Dean Bryce Sullivan and David Curtis, English Department Chair. The staff of Belmont's Bunch Library including Paige Carter and Nicole Fox were very helpful to me in locating unusual British books and articles. Katherine Hansen, my former student in Wisconsin and current friend, read an early draft of this book and encouraged me to keep writing better, more accurate accounts of each adventure. Joseph Pearce, scholar extraordinaire, inspired me to keep reading, writing, and learning more about the broad and deep traditions of Christian liberal humanism and the path of the *homo viator* or "itinerate person." Claudia of course was my first inspiration and eagerly supported this project all the way, including the long days of walking between villages in the rain. My family Jon, Terra, Bodhi, Libby, Nick, Henry, Margie, and Ruben were very interested and wanted updates. To each and every person who took an interest in this book, I am overflowing with gratitude and thankfulness.

Jonathan Thorndike teaches writing and literature at Belmont University. He previously published two books on American history and over 50 essays on Japanese and British literature. Thorndike's book *Epperson vs. Arkansas* won a state library book-of-the-year award,

Jonathan and Claudia Thorndike live in Nashville, Tennessee.